A
N
S
P
A
C
E

MANSPACE

A PRIMAL GUIDE TO MARKING YOUR TERRITORY

SAM MARTIN

The Taunton Press

Text © 2006 by Sam Martin

Photographs ©Marco Prozzo: pp. ii, 6 (right), 11 (top left), 28-30, 172-175, 204–206; ©Brian Vanden Brink: pp. vi (bottom left), 2, 36-39, 83 (bottom), 119 (right), 159 (right); ©Ken Gutmaker: pp. vi (top right), 51 (top), 56-59, 102-104, 110-111, 140-143, 161 (right), 180-183, 208–211; ©Eric Roth: pp. vi (bottom & center right), 12, 15 (top & right), 83 (top); ©Rob Karosis: pp. 3 (right), 50, 60-63, 82 (top), 90-93, 144–147, 186–189, 212–215; ©Denise Prince Martin: pp. 4 (bottom), 68–71, 152-155; Tim Street Porter: pp. 5 (left), 10 (top right), 80–81; ©Matthew Benson: pp. 5 (top right), 126–128, 166–168; ©Simon Upton, The Interior Archive, Inc.: p. 5 (bottom); ©Carolyn L. Bates: pp. 6 (left), 7, 21, 48, 94–98, 100–101, 158, 184–185, 196–203; ©Shooting Star Archives: pp. 8 (top), Viacom, Shooting Star Archives (bottom), 9 Roman Salicki, Shooting Star Archives, (top right); ©Elvis Presley Enterprises, Inc.: p. 9 (left); ©Marc Samu: pp. 10 (bottom), 118–119, 121 (left); ©Audrey Hall: pp. 11 (top right), 161 (top), 164–165, 170–170, 190–193; ©Andrew Garn: pp. 14 (left), 15 (bottom left), 40–41; courtesy The McKernon Group, Inc.: pp. 14 (top), 46–47; Janice Rubin, courtesy The Orange Show Center for Visionary Art: p. 15 (bottom right); ©Randy O'Rourke: pp. 16, 18–20, 22–27, 52–54, 136–139; ©Sydney Brink: pp. 33–35; ©Jason Meyer: pp. 42–43, 48–49, 51 (right); Great Hunters, courtesy Safari Press: pp. 44–45; ©Christopher Simon Sykes, The Interior Archive: pp. 50 (left), 120 (top right), 121 (right); Amy Albert, courtesy The Taunton Press, Inc., pp. 64–67; ©Gary Reighn: pp. 72–73; ©Ben Fink: pp. 50 (top), 74–76; courtesy Good Times Stove Co.: p. 77; ©George Reps: pp. 78–79; Burt Stout, courtesy David Ballinger: pp. 82 (left), 116–117; ©Nick Wheeler: p. 83 (left); ©Joseph Kugielsky: pp. 84–87; Charles Bickford, courtesy The Taunton Press, Inc.: pp. 88–89; ©James Ray Spahn: pp. 106–107, 109; ©Nelson Sharp: p. 108; ©Nicole Whitten: pp. 112–114, 160 (left); Loeb H. Granoff, courtesy Harry S. Truman Library: p. 115 (top); courtesy The Little White House, Key West, FL.: p. 115 (bottom); ©Fritz von der Schulenburg, The Interior Archive: pp. 120 (left), 121 (bottom right); ©Barry Beck: pp. 122–125; ©Charles Mayer: pp. 132–133; ©Chris Faust: pp. 134–135; Richard Sprengler, courtesy Rocio Romero, LLC, Designer: pp. 148–150; ©Povy Kendal Martin: pp. 156–157, 194–195; ©Andrea Rugg: pp. 162–163; ©Scott Zimmerman: pp. 176–178; Mitch McComb, courtesy Hank Louis: p. 179

Illustrations © 2006 by The Taunton Press, Inc.

The Taunton Press, Inc., 63 South Main Street, PO Box 5506, Newtown, CT 06470-5506

e-mail: tp@taunton.com

Editor: Erica Sanders-Foege

Jacket/Cover and Interior design: Chika Azuma

Illustrator: Scott Bricher

Front cover photographs: ©Brian Vanden Brink (top right), Charles Bickford, courtesy The Taunton Press (middle right), ©Marco Prozzo (bottom right), ©Ken Gutmaker (top left), ©Denise Prince Martin (middle left)

Back cover photographs: ©Andrew Garn (top left), ©Bob Ginder Studio (bottom left)

Author photograph: ©Denise Prince Martin

Spine photograph: © Marco Prozzo

Library of Congress Cataloging-in-Publication Data

Martin, Sam.
  Manspace : a primal guide to marking your territory / Sam Martin
     p. cm.
  ISBN-13: 978-1-56158-820-6
  ISBN-10: 1-56158-820-2
  1. Interior architecture. 2. Personal space. 3. Men--Attitudes. I. Title.
  NA2850.M375 2006
  729--dc22
                          2006006545

Printed in China
10 9 8 7 6 5 4 3 2 1

The following manufacturers/names appearing in *Manspace* are trademarks: Airstream®, Alesis®, Astroturf®, Bakelite®, Barbie®, BMW®, Bugati®, Crown®, Ducati®, Electro-Voice®, Fiestaware®, Garland®, Gibson®, Guinness®, Hot Wheels®, Hula-Popper®, Lexan®, MatchBox®, Microsoft®, Mini Cooper®, Nerf®, Neumann®, Nike®, Pac-Man®, Performer®, Philco Predicta®, Playboy Mansion℠, Plexiglas®, Ping-Pong®, Saab®, Saturn®, Schmidt-Cassegrain Meade®, Vespa®, X-Box®, Yamaha®

For Ford and Wren, my inspiration throughout

ACKNOWLEDGMENTS

Despite all the solitary work that comes along with the writing life, this book never would have made it off the press without the work of quite a few people.

Thanks to editor Steve Culpepper for picking up the phone in the first place and offering inspired direction before and during the project. Photo researcher Jen Matlack tracked down most of the locations in the book and deserves a huge thank you. As does project editor Robyn Doyon-Aitken, who kept everything in order and on track better than I ever could. Also, I'd like to give a hearty shout-out to my editor Erica Sanders-Foege for sharing my vision for the book and for offering excellent guidance through the dog days.

I'd also like to thank my wife, Denise, and my two boys, Ford and Wren, for the love, support, and laughter they offered through countless late nights and a few lost weekends. None of this would be possible without you.

And last, thanks to all the guys who shared their spaces and endured my prying questions. I hope your example can inspire.

TABLE OF CONTENTS

ONE

IT'S A MAN'S, MAN'S,

AN'S, MAN'S WORLD

"A man cannot be comfortable without his own approval." — *Mark Twain*

Whoever said "a man's home is his castle" didn't get it quite right. We might unclog the toilet when it overflows, mow the yard when the grass gets high, or even pay the mortgage once a month. But castle? That implies we get to do whatever we want in the house, and that's just not true. Anyone who has ever lived with a wife, kids, or live-in girlfriend can tell you that.

In fact, a more accurate adage might be, "A man's home is his castle until his significant other moves in." For it's then that we lose control. Table saws and tools in the garage get crowded out by bicycles and soccer gear. Motorcycle posters are replaced by Impressionist prints. The college leg lamp is banished. Before we know it, the only space left is a bedside table or the top of a dresser—just enough room for the contents of our pockets.

Lately though, men have started to find freedom where they can. Backyards, spare bedrooms, unfinished attics, old outbuildings or brand new buildings have all been taken over with a new found sense of purpose.

I built my manspace—a 165-sq.-ft. shed in the backyard—after writing my first book at a desk in the living room. My oldest son was two at the time and was just learning how to reach onto the top of the desk to pull the keyboard off. Papers stacked up and my wife let me know about it. And, of course, when anyone wanted to sit in the living room they'd have to contend with me, my deadline, and my bad attitude. I finished the book, but two years later when we were expecting our second child and I was working on another big project I knew it was time to get out of the house. There was a spare patch of ground in the backyard so I went to work. Five months, $3,000, and a few banged-up fingernails later I had a writing space that was all mine.

MALE BY DESIGN

This book is about those spaces men have staked out for themselves. Some are elegantly designed, whereas others are uniquely handmade. There's a photography studio in a barn, an English-style pub in a basement, and a ten-pin bowling alley in a backyard. One guy built a home office inside a grain silo, whereas another constructed a Japanese tearoom over his garage.

What men do in their own spaces is as important as the spaces themselves. Hobbies and professions are realized there, as are fun and games. In fact, it's often the activity that defines the manspace. One collector near Sag Harbor, N.Y., had amassed a small museum's worth of 18th- and

Serious hobbyists have serious manspaces, like this wood-paneled wine cellar built with climate control and storage for hundreds of bottles.

For lots of guys their cars are the only places they can call their own. Writer Bill Kerby created an homage to previous manspaces with this birdhouse.

By stocking his 19th-century photography studio with period antiques, Matthew Benson proves that not all men will stack beer-can pyramids when given their own place.

Not everyone has a huge library to play with. Most of us have to carve something out wherever we can.

19th-century nautical antiques before his wife told him they couldn't stay in the house. So he used a room over the garage and re-created the inside of a 150-year-old British Naval man-o'-war to store the collection. Whether men are storing things, playing with trains, pouring pints, watching the game, or cutting 2x4s, there's a space to fit the need.

Now that I have a place of my own, I have that crucial separation between work and home. Twenty steps from my back door to the office doesn't sound like much, but it's miles away from what I had before. I get up and have breakfast with the family. Then I tell everyone goodbye as if I'm about to get in the car and drive in rush-hour traffic to some distant job. My wife and the kids happily play along because they remember the desk and the tension in the living room. We've also come up with a set of unwritten laws: When dad's "at work" no one is allowed in the room. Of course, it's always nice to take a break and throw the baseball with my sons or have lunch with my wife—the luxuries of working at home. But it's equally as nice to get back to work and know that I am the master of my domain.

After finding the two sets of 8-ft.-high French doors at a Habitat for Humanity Re-Store, I built the office—essentially a box with a shed roof—using nothing but a circular saw and a hammer.

With room to spare in the back-yard, I had the space outside if not inside to build my own office. Now the commute is short and the main house is committed to living not working.

Inside the office, I covered the walls and ceiling with ¼-in. wood paneling and installed some simple bracketed bookshelves. It might be spare, but it's all mine.

A Brief History of Men's Spaces

The desire to create our own spaces starts at a very young age. Almost as soon as we were able to walk we were draping sheets over chairs for an indoor hideout or leaning sticks against a fence for a backyard fort. Tree houses came later with help from dad, who no doubt considered making the platform strong enough to hold him, too. In fact, it may be that these childhood experiences are what make it so hard for grown men to accept not having much more room than the hall closet.

At one time men really were kings of their castles—literally. Of course, that was more for security reasons than the need to invite friends over for the World Series. Still, those men didn't have anyone telling them to drain the moat or suggesting that they move their thrones to a less visible section of the house. Somewhere along the way, control changed hands.

Perhaps it all started during the Industrial Revolution, when men started leaving home every day for long hours in the factory or at the office, making the job a man's space more than a castle. But even in the early 20th century, when the Industrial Revolution was in full swing, it was common for men to "retire to the drawing room" together to light up some cigars, drink scotch, and talk business and politics—topics that were considered too weighty for women's ears. That would suggest that social customs, at least, demanded that men have their own spaces.

By the 1950s the only areas of the house that were

Since the 1950s men have tolerated the car, the kids' gear, and the overflow storage to setup shop in the garage. Now they're branching out.

The garage has long been set aside as a man-only space. Rob Harrison's Seattle car park houses his motorcycles, while his wife's car must face the elements.

This man couldn't get a space of his own so he turned to the hall closet—with typically messy results.

Part garage, part laboratory, and part hideout, Batman and Robin's Batcave is what man-space dreams are made of.

Archie Bunker may not have been the master of his domain on the TV show *All in the Family*, but his throne was untouchable.

considered men's spaces were the ones that were unin-habitable—and therefore immune to interior decoration and a weekly cleaning. Basements, attics, and garages were available for the hobbyist or tinkerer as long as he didn't mind working in uninsulated, dusty, or dank spots next to the furnace or the car. Garages especially became a distinctly male domain. That's where the car was parked (and worked on). It was also where a man kept his tools, his lawn mower, and, if he was lucky, his workbench. The problem with the garage or any other unfinished space attached to the house was that it was also considered a storage space. Inevitably, men lost ground to a growing collection of domestic stuff.

The latter half of the 20th century was not a good time for male dominion. There was the onset of the femi-nist revolution. Whatever rooms men had comfortably called their own were taken away from them once and for all. It wasn't that women took over the garages and base-ments of the world; it's just that they no longer tolerated men working in them. Instead, husbands and boyfriends were expected to help clean the house, cook dinner, and raise the kids. And with two working parents, what choice did they have?

CLASSIC MANSPACES

As men's spaces shrunk, their legend grew in the popular culture. As early as the 1940s, Superman comics were sketching out the man of steel's Fortress of Solitude. This "secret citadel" is where the superhero could "retire to shut out the world for a short time." There was a super labora-tory, an intergalactic zoo, and a separate apartment for when Supergirl was in town. On television shows like *The Brady Bunch*, Mike Brady had a home office that was off limits to the rest of the household. Later, Batman and Robin showed up on the scene with their Batcave, an electronic, gadget-rich garage any guy would dream of having. There was John Belushi and his frat brothers in the movie *Animal House*, which featured one of the defining men-only party pads of the generation. Even Archie Bunker had his chair—a small but undeniable manspace.

GRACELAND

How close any of the TV shows or movies mentioned here came to real life is questionable, though in some cases life does imitate art. One man and his manspace that have become part of the cultural fabric of the country is Elvis and his Memphis mansion, Graceland. The King's 23-room house features a TV room, a music room, a billiard room, a racquetball court, and a trophy room to display his gold records. He even put a waterfall in one space and called it a jungle room. Perhaps more impressive than any of the rooms in the house is the fact that Elvis managed to do all this while living with his wife, mother, and grandmother all under the same roof. One can understand how the women in his life allowed the music and trophy rooms. He was, after all, the King of Rock and Roll. It's also possible to imagine how he convinced his wife to let him add a billiard room so that he and the band could wind down after a session. How he got the jungle room approved, though, boggles the mind.

THE PLAYBOY MANSION

Bachelors and their pads—or what I call "total manspaces"—have always managed a larger than life look. In fact, not a few married men have looked upon the sunken living rooms, shag carpets, and black matte finishes of their unmarried brethren with a touch of jealousy, and none more so than bachelor number one Hugh Hefner and his manspace of all manspaces, the Playboy Mansion℠.

Purchased for just over $1 million in 1971, Hef's six-acre 30-room Shangri-La in Los Angeles boasts an indoor cavelike pool room, a master bedroom with sound and light controls on the headboard, a bathroom with a black marble tub in the middle of the room, and a closet larger than some New York apartments. The parties held in the mansion are infamous. Along with countless celebrities swimming, drinking, and schmoozing, these rooms have been host to more cleavage than a Hollywood tanning salon. As Peter O'Toole once quipped about the space, "This is what God would have done if He'd had the money."

Hugh Hefner uses one of the Playboy Mansion's 22 bedrooms to pore over images for the next issue of the magazine he started in 1953.

The TV room at Graceland was set up so Elvis could watch triple the football action on Sundays. The mirrored walls also housed the King's hi-fi equipment and collection of 45s.

Creating a Room of Your Own

In a way, the bachelor pad may be the easiest type of manspace to invent. After all, bachelors live alone; they have no choice but to have their own space. Those who live with others have a far more challenging task ahead of them.

For those guys, getting a manspace starts with targeting a location. It could be the garage or an unfinished basement—it's been done before so why not again. Some lock in on a little-used guest room, a back porch, or even a corner of the backyard. No matter if it's 1,000 sq. ft. or 100 sq. ft., like Jay Shafer's minihouse, a man will

make the best of what he's got. Often, the best time to grab a space is during a house move, when your wife or girlfriend is preoccupied with other things. In these cases you'll need to move fast and be decisive. That's what John Morgan did in Austin, Texas. As soon as the moving truck pulled up he grabbed a box of his stuff and took it straight to an old carriage house on his new property that he wanted to turn into a saloon. Before his wife realized what was going on he'd already put half a dozen boxes in there and unpacked a string of Christmas lights. She was too tired to argue about it and four years later even she calls it the man house.

When you can't get the jump on a space like Morgan did, you may need to talk to your significant other to make the case for a manspace. First off, it's important to explain what it is you plan to do in your own room or building. After all, a manspace is more than just tacking

Sometimes all it takes is a hammock and a spare corner of the porch for a man to have a place of his own to read and wind down on the weekends.

Once you carve out one room or out-building, why stop there? Montana's Charlie Ringer started with a workshop; now he has a fenced compound with three buildings.

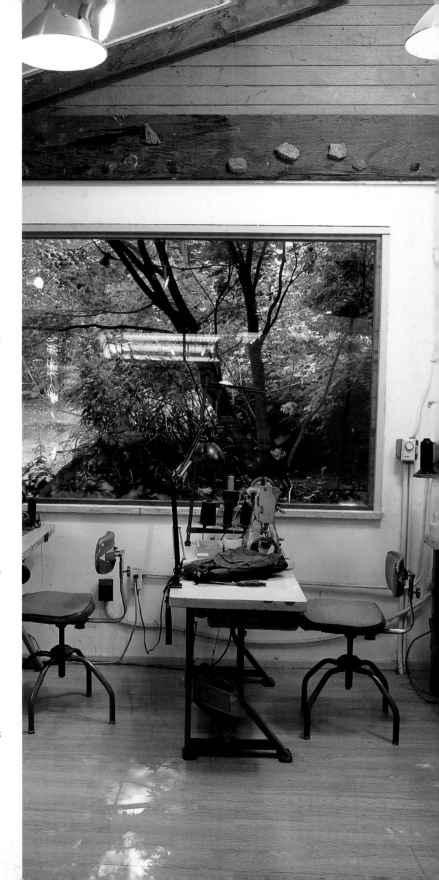

Collecting things is a great way to get your own space, if only because one day your wife or girlfriend will get tired of looking at things like your model roadster collection.

up a few posters and moving in some dark wood furniture. If it's work you want to do, talk about the money you can make or the things you can build—for her—with a dedicated room of your own. Sports and music fans can make the case that a manspace would get the entertainment center out of the living room—always a popular argument. Then again, there are those who don't have to do much convincing at all. In fact, most guys who collect things are often urged to find some other place to keep their stuff. (There isn't a woman in the world who wouldn't be glad to see a collection of animal skulls or old radios hidden from plain sight.)

Once the space is secured, there are no rules for how to set it up or any color palettes to work by. Most men just know what to do and when to do it. If not, they give it time. Stuff will collect, friends will leave things behind, and the space will become the outward expression of who they are and what they do. After all, the manspaces we create have less to do with the space itself and more to do with the man inside.

Home offices and studios like David Kimura's backpack-making shop have been men-only domains for as long as men have worked.

"Too much is never enough." — *Morris Lapidus*

It's impossible to gauge when men first started collecting stuff—an Inuit hunter may have socked away a few walrus tusks in his igloo shed as early as 2000 B.C. What most experts agree on, however, is that the urge starts young and takes shape during the college years in the form of a beer-can pyramid. Even after, some guys still can't bring themselves to recycle their empties—witness the Beer Can House in Houston, Tex., a structure sided in roughly 39,000 cans collected over an 18-year period by John Milkovisch, a retired railroad employee with a taste for hops. Milkovisch notwithstanding, most men do manage to branch out, gathering, hording, and storing everything from lunch pails to race cars. Of course, men and their stuff have been the source of untold amounts of conjugal strife and breakups. One can almost hear the words now: "Either the action figures go, or I do."

And so it is that men who collect have created manspaces in which to store their collections. Though these rooms and outbuildings do serve the same utilitarian purpose as that of a storage unit, most also double as giant display cases. Here guys can keep their stuff and show it off. For that reason, some collectors' spaces inevitably become full-fledged hangouts, home offices, and workshops all in one—a slight distortion of the space's original purpose, but who's counting?

One 60-year-old collector of fishing tackle in Missouri keeps his guitar and amp stashed between boxes of Egyptian Wobbler lures and stacks of Indiana reels. In New York City, a photographer has stuffed so many cameras, radios, clocks, and other gear into his 500-sq.-ft. apartment that he no longer has any room to have friends over. Another, a wild-game hunter, is building an indoor mountain diorama over 50 ft. high on which to position his collection of more than 300 specimens.

Whatever it is men decide to collect is as varied as the manspaces they create to put it in. In this chapter you'll see all kinds of gear—antique toys, motorcycles, fishing lures, model trains, and stuffed animal heads—housed in everything from a spare bedroom to a grass-roofed garage to a recording studio. As you read through these pages you'll realize that when it comes to collecting, nothing is off limits. Maybe now you'll give in to your urge to start gathering—and displaying—something of your own.

Manspace Ho!

Men always rise to a challenge, especially if it presents a threat to their collectibles. After this man's wife told him his 18th- and 19th-century nautical antiques could no longer stay in their New York City apartment, he moved everything to their weekend home near Sag Harbor on Long Island. It seemed appropriate for the model ships and sailor's gear to be next to one of the country's most historic port towns anyway. But as soon as the couple began spending more time on Long Island, the collection came under fire again. The violent history infused in the whaling harpoons freaked his wife out, he says. Faced with total rejection, the man turned to his only option: He built a manspace.

What kind of a room does a man build for nautical antiques? One that looks like the inside of a ship, of course. The 20-ft. by 40-ft. room features a central "mast," port-hole windows, some of which are 150 years old, and wood-plank walls. Lest anyone think the room is a purely impractical indulgence, there is a two-car garage underneath.

If it were taken aboard a ship in the 18th century, this guy owns it, including ball-and-powder pistols, a British marine uniform, trunks, telescopes, and a captain's log from 1780.

This ship's wheel is from an 1810 Royal Navy ship. The brass object at left is a large binnacle or compass.

Old whaling harpoons lean against the wall next to several model ships. The collector has about 15 models that date back to the 1850s and one from 1730.

Long fascinated by the lives of men who have lived and worked at sea, this collector has been gathering seafaring paraphernalia for 40 years. As a child he spent many summers on Cape Cod and in Montauk, N.Y., staring at the boats and sailing with whoever would take him out. By 18, he had his first collectible—an old ship model. Ever since, he has hunted for nautical treasures everywhere he goes, which could be to Hong Kong, Singapore, or other international ports of call that he visits for his job as a crisis manager and communication specialist. The result is a museum-quality collection of over 400 objects dating from the early 1700s to about 1870.

THE GOLDEN AGE OF SAILING

According to the collector, his antiques come from what he calls the "golden age of sailing," when England's Royal Navy ruled the sea, the American whaling industry peaked, and pirates became legendary. His collection includes things from each of those three groups of seamen. In one corner of the room he has a Royal Marine uniform and military gear from British warships. In another is a pirate's galley, complete with ale bottles and cast-iron treasure chests. There's even a ship's wheel, 150-year-old models of whaling ships, and a 19th-century diving helmet.

Now that the space is set up, he spends time up there reading books or tinkering with his things. On occasion he'll even work there. Because he's confident the collection is complete, he rarely buys new items for the room. He does still look, though, just in case he runs across that one item he can't live without.

The pirate's corner features two cast-iron safe boxes. The one on the floor weighs 400 lb.—thought to be too heavy to steal—and has a secret keyhole and compartment in which to stash the key.

Seamen of the 19th century first used diving helmets like this one to clean the bottom of ships or recover lost booty. The glass balls wrapped in netting are Japanese fishing floats. Even the barrels date to the 1800s.

MISTER MICROPHONE

Some guys like to preserve their collections on shelves or in glass display cases where they can't be disturbed. Not Chas Eller. When musicians like Shawn Colvin or Doc Watson walk into his studio in Vermont to record a new song, he'll pull out five or six microphones from his personal stash to see which one sounds the best. It could be an old Neumann® tube mike from World War II, an RCA® ribbon mike from the late 1960s, or a solid-state microphone he bought five years ago. Each one brings a unique sound, and it's up to Eller to determine which mike is best for the song he plans to record.

Eller has been collecting microphones since becoming a recording engineer in 1977. In the 1980s he played keyboards for the jazz band Kilimanjaro and started picking up mikes to record his own songs. Now he is by no means finished collecting. For Eller, the mike is the most important part of the recording process, and no amount of equipment can take its place.

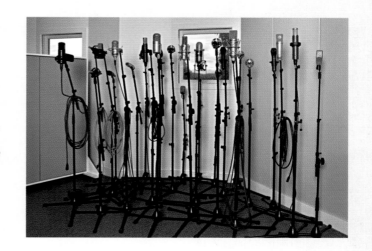

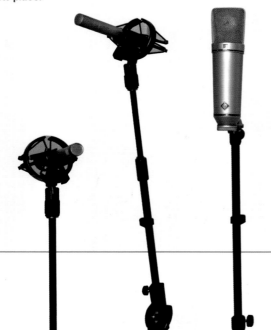

Renaissance Man on the Hudson

For artists, the creative process is crucial to how their art turns out. Some can only work late at night. Others have to have loud music blaring. Most have to have their own space. Like artist Robert Ginder. He also needs his collection of odd knickknacks to jump-start his imagination and provide some ever-valuable comic relief.

Ginder and his wife Cara live in the Hudson Valley not far from New York City. Their house is a former boardinghouse and grocery store, so there are plenty of extra rooms. For his studio Ginder took two old parlor rooms as well as the entire ground floor, which is where the store used to be. His collection of oddities, like a saber-toothed tiger skull, vials of honey, and a 1930s-era prosthetic hand, are arranged carefully throughout.

Ginder hasn't always had such a great setup. He and Cara, who is also an artist, lived and worked together in a TriBeCa loft in New York City. The loft was one giant room with half set aside for living and half for painting—not the

The Ginders' house was built onto the side of an ancient rock outcrop in the 18th century. In Bob's Moroccan-themed ground-floor studio, the entire back wall is ledge.

Ginder's landscape paintings (like the one picture here) and his fondness for objects used by naturalists and explorers is reminiscent of the 19th-century Hudson River School painters.

Ginder's wonderfully weird collection of objects includes a saber-toothed tiger skull, an ostrich egg, a romanticized bronze statue of Rembrandt, and a tiny model of Picasso's head.

best situation for two artists with different creative routines. "She worked at one end of the room and I sat at the other, and we would listen to different music at the same time pretending not to hear each other," he says. Still, the arrangement worked well enough for several years.

SPACE TO FILL

Then, in 1996, Cara gave birth to their daughter Charlotte. They tried to keep up their work schedules in the city, but after three years the place just became too small and they decided to move upstate. They bought their current house mostly because they liked the scenery, but also because it offered plenty of room for Ginder to spread out his collectibles and get to work.

Ginder collects unusual objects to amuse himself, but also to use in his artwork. He found three 150-year-old

Two of Ginder's guitars—
a Dobro-style resonator guitar
and a hollow-body Gibson® copy—
sit on stands in the upstairs parlor.
Behind them is a folding screen
made to look like a bookcase.

Downstairs, Ginder displays his art atop a bank of chemist's drawers. He writes poetry, cuts it up or erases it, and stores the remnants in marble containers, glass vials, and test tubes.

frames at a local antique shop and painted landscapes for them in the style of the 19th-century Hudson River School. Another time, he ran across some old glass chemist's bottles and a collection of rock vials. He used those to store bits of poems he had written, along with pencil shavings and eraser rubbings. In one of the other rooms that Ginder paints in, he spreads objects out on the mantelpiece or on tables like a Victorian naturalist. There's a fake human skull, a whale harpoon, measuring instruments, and old fountain pens. All of Ginder's things come from local antique stores and flea markets.

On Thursday nights, Ginder, also a musician, invites a few friends over to play jazz. They usually gather upstairs around the piano, which is Ginder's instrument of choice, but sometimes they'll play downstairs in the old grocery store. During the days, Ginder makes art and prepares for gallery shows in New York and Los Angeles. He might use all four rooms by dinner time, painting in one, building frames in another, and searching through his things for research in the other two. It's a process he values as much as his finished paintings.

♀ VICTORY LAP
A PAINTER'S WORK

Robert Ginder collects curious antiques for fun, but he's serious about his painting. After a brief college stint, Ginder apprenticed with a few artists but largely taught himself the techniques he uses today. He paints still lifes of fruit, palm trees, and the West Coast bungalows he grew up with in California. He paints in gold leaf on wood surfaces that are rounded at the top, so his work resembles early Renaissance religious icons.

A Motorcycle Man's Garage

Before getting a garage of his own, architect Rob Harrison parked his motorcycles in a walk-in basement. There was a garage on the property, but it was hardly big enough for the couple's car, much less Rob's two-wheelers and the tools he uses to work on them. Because the place was a rental, he and his wife didn't renovate.

When it came time for the Harrisons to buy a house in 2003, Rob's foremost condition was that it had to have a garage big enough for his bikes. Unfortunately, the house they fell in love with near downtown Seattle only had a carport, which was in terrible shape. They bought the house anyway. Rob realized that he'd get to design and build his own eco-friendly garage.

TIME TO MOW THE ROOF

Rather than just tearing down the carport and deck and carting it off to the dump, Harrison carefully took the place apart board by board so he could reuse the lumber. The foundation was solid, so he took the 2×6 treated lumber from the old deck and used it to frame out the garage walls right on the existing slab. For the garage roof he planned to install a 3-in. layer of sod atop the old roof sheathing salvaged from the carport. To support the added weight of the dirt and plant life—a "green" roof—Harrison brought in some 1½-in. by 9½-in. laminated veneer lumber beams that span the entire length of the space. For siding he used unpainted fiber

The "green" roof of Harrison's garage has been covered with dirt and planted with grasses and sedums to blend with the surrounding landscape and provide additional insulation.

Rob Harrison's eco-friendly garage holds his three motorcycles: a Ducatti® 900 Super Sport, a 1978 Yamaha® SR 500, and a 1986 BMW® R80 G/S Paris Dakar, which he rides to work.

cement panels and sealed plywood. After three months, the space was complete at a cost of about $20,000.

Now Harrison has a place to park his motorbikes and tinker with them. During the renovation he ran electricity to the space to power lights and tools and he added an outdoor water spigot to make washing the machines easy. Pegboard stocked with hand tools lines the walls, as does a budding collection of motorcycle posters. He lets his wife park her car there on occasion, but only because she drives a Mini Cooper®, which doesn't take up too much space. If it did, he'd have to remind her that in his space two wheels trump four.

Rob Harrison's three-year-old son Rowan is getting an early introduction to the benefits of having a dedicated space in which to wield fixed wrenches.

Motorcycle racing posters cover the wall over Harrison's BMW touring bike—the one he rode to Alaska along the rough and tumble Cassiar Highway.

To construct a "green" roof system, Harrison first beefed up the roof structure to compensate for the added weight of the dirt (his 280-sq.-ft. roof has 3 in. of soil on it, adding 17 lb. per sq. ft.). He sealed the roof decking with an ice and water shield. On top of that went a single-ply plastic membrane, then a geotextile filter fabric that creates a stable base and helps control erosion. Harrison added metal flashing, which also helps contain the dirt, around the edge of the roof and down over the fascia.

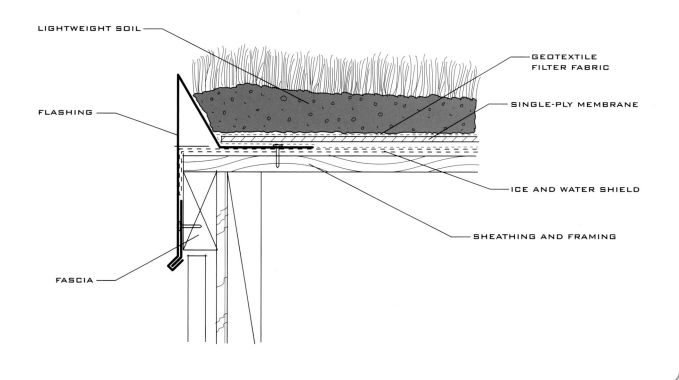

LIGHTWEIGHT SOIL

GEOTEXTILE FILTER FABRIC

FLASHING

SINGLE-PLY MEMBRANE

ICE AND WATER SHIELD

SHEATHING AND FRAMING

FASCIA

A Fish Tale

Like many collectors, retired postal worker and amateur bass angler Larry Moellman didn't necessarily claim his manspace as much as his stuff did. In his possession is a vast collection of antique and unusual fish trophies, minnow buckets, rods, reels, and lures—especially lures—many of which have the box or tin in which they were originally sold. The superannuated hooks, made out of glass, plastic, or wood, have names like Wizard Wiggler and Hula-Popper®. It didn't take long for Moellman's wife Connie to suggest that he take his stuff far away from her and put it in a spare bedroom in their 1880 farmhouse in Camp Cole, Miss.

Moellman didn't realize it at the time, but he started collecting in 1985, the year his father passed away and left Moellman his fishing tackle. The two had fished together since Moellman was a boy, so he held on to it for sentimental reasons. But after several sightings of antique equipment at local flea markets and garage sales he began to enjoy finding unusual or rare gear. Before long he was hooked, so to speak, and he began collecting seriously. When his wife suggested putting his finds in the spare bedroom he jumped at the chance.

Larry Moellman in his Missouri manspace holding an antique Chinese rod and reel and surrounded by his collection of fishing tackle.

A ROOM ONLY HE COULD LOVE

Over the years Moellman has remodeled the inside of the room to look like an old country bait shop. He paneled the walls and trimmed the doors and windows with fading red barn wood he salvaged with a friend, and then created a wainscoting out of sections of fake brick. To imitate the look of exposed ceiling joists he installed some box beams and painted them the same faded red as the walls. In addition to making shelves and glass display cases for the collectibles, he's managed to squeeze in a desk, a computer, a stereo system, and a few chairs for when his friends stop by.

Only once has Moellman tried to expand his man-space to other areas of the house. When he and Connie were remodeling the kitchen he made a display of all red and white lures—"red and white are her favorite colors," he says—and suggested that they might look good hanging on the wall. "She said, 'Just turn around and go back to your room,'" says Moellman. After that he never tried again. "I'm allowed only this one room," he says. And that could be his most prized possession of all.

YOU CAN USE ONE LIVE MINNOW ALL DAY

German Silver Fittings

German Silver Fittings

PATENT PENDING

GEAR
THE ONE THAT GOT AWAY

Larry Moellman collects fishing equipment from all over the world, but his favorite tackle came from three states away—in Michigan. That's where, in 1914, the Detroit Glass Minnow Company manufactured a test-tube-like glass lure that could house a live minnow, thereby tricking larger fish into getting caught on one of four treble hooks. "You were supposed to be able to use only one minnow all day long," says Moellman. "Instead, everyone kept breaking the lure on rocks, tree stumps, and the side of the boat. That's why they're so hard to find now."

Moellman collects all the lures of a certain color or company before selling them and starting on another. It keeps his interest high, his room organized, and his stuff out of the rest of the house.

Classic Car Club

Boston native Andy Rheault bought his first car when he was 8 years old and his second when he was 14. By age 72 he had bought and sold hundreds of different types of cars. However, his most fervent passion for the internal combustion engine was reserved for the Italian-designed Bugatti® sports car. According to his wife Sarah, Andy was the world's foremost authority on the Bugatti, an auto that first made a name for itself in the Italian and Monaco Grand Prix races in the teens and twenties. He edited *Pur Sang*, the quarterly magazine from the American Bugatti Club, and he raced the vintage autos in events around the world.

In his later years, Rheault (pronounced "row") moved to Maine with Sarah, also an auto enthusiast, and converted an old barn into a garage for his cars. The two-story building dates to 1870 and had dirt floors when the Rheaults first bought it. Andy had a concrete floor poured, took out half the second story, and had

Andy Rheault's 19th-century barn has room enough for cars of all sizes, including the red 1959 Morris Minor in the back on the left and the 1927 Type 52 battery-powered Bugatti made for kids.

OBSCOT BOAT WORKS

Though he gutted the 1870 barn, Rheault kept its original columns. The loft upstairs was used as a reading library stocked with car magazines.

All cars in the Rheault collection are serviced in a separate workshop. The seats on this 1926 Type 13 Bugatti have been removed to access the battery.

several walls removed to create one giant room with a loft. He also added two sets of bifold doors opposite the barn's original entryway so the cars could be driven in and out from both sides. To keep oil and engine grease out of the showroom, Andy used a separate workshop adjacent to the barn to stock tools and parts for regular maintenance work.

After Andy passed away in 2000, Sarah kept some of the cars. Their son kept Rheault's 1960 Porsche 356B. Others were willed to friends. At age 66, Sarah continues to race one of the Bugattis, as Andy would have. At the end of the day, the car goes back to the space he made for it.

Andrew Garn thinks collecting is in his blood. "My mother collected stuff, now I do," says the 48-year-old photographer. He also thinks it's a problem. The New York apartment where he displays his finds is a mere 500 sq. ft., hardly big enough to accommodate his habit. Plus, with all the shelves, stacks, and display tables in addition to his office, there isn't much room for entertaining.

But still he keeps gathering, unable to fend off the desire to own things when he visits museums or travels to various countries and cities, which he does often for work. Rather than focus on pursuing a single item or theme—a skill he admires in other collectors—Garn picks whatever catches his eye. He'll group things and then separate them into various subgroups he defines as technical, architectural, medical, or photographic, to name a few.

Presently Garn is into colorful paraphernalia from the golden age of science fiction. In the past, though, he's gone through plants, matchbox cars, baseball cards, and animal skulls. He started buying Bakelite® radios from the 1940s and 1950s 20 years ago for 25 cents a pop at yard sales. Now he gets most of his things at auctions and antique markets, like the one on Chicago's Randolph Street.

Back at his East Village apartment, Garn is very conscious of taking care of his collection. He dusts regularly and culls merchandise when things start to get too cluttered (he has started transferring items to a small weekend cabin). Rather than just buying things and hording them, he uses his collection as decoration throughout the apartment. That way if he ever manages to find room to entertain guests, they'll have some interesting things to look at.

Andrew Garn's Manhattan apartment holds a collection of Art Deco furniture, mid-century radios, folk art, and a 1958 Philco Predicta® television that was rented out for a TV ad.

What started off as the need for a simple alarm clock grew into a mid-century George Nelson clock collection that adorns the bookshelf and wall of Garn's bedroom.

Garn started coveting old cameras like the plastic Diana, which he still uses, after seeing another camera collection in a photography museum outside of Paris.

A Manspace in Search of Some Men

In a world where men's spaces are divided between the "haves" and "have-nots," it will come as no surprise that some of the "haves" have more than they need. Luxury homebuilder Paul T. Schumacher is one of these men. In the walk-out basement of his 12,000-sq.-ft. Ohio home where he lives with his wife and two young children, Schumacher has a veritable surplus of manspace. There's a bar with six bar stools, a home theater, a standard-size racquetball court, and, next to the fireplace, a pool table. If that isn't enough, one can also find a wine cellar big enough to hold up to 600 bottles of wine, a dining room

table, and an oversize cigar humidor. Schumacher doesn't actually collect wine, aside from several dozen bottles he keeps on hand for parties. Nor does he smoke cigars. Still, he could if he wanted to.

PARTY CENTRAL

Until then, the room is ripe with potential. The door to the room features cigar-shaped pulls. There's also a tiny window in the door similar to what you'd find in some back-alley speakeasy. That way whoever is on the inside can get a look at whoever comes a knockin'—perfect for when you need to talk to your wife but you don't want her to see how much cash you've lost or how much whiskey you've downed in that evening's poker game.

Wine can be stored in four arched alcoves. In one there's a cigar humidor to preserve several boxes of finely rolled tobacco. To chill a large wine collection—when Schumacher gets one—the room has a separate cooling system. It also features a commercial-grade ventilation system to keep cigar smoke from wafting into the next room. Schumacher has begun testing the room's potential by having buddies over to play poker, uncork a few bottles, and smoke cigars. Before that, his was just a manspace waiting to happen.

Props inside the room set an authentic stage for a perfectly smoky and boozy good time—as soon as Schumacher decides to invite his buddies over more often.

Like a movie set waiting for actors, Paul Schumacher's little-used wine and cigar room waits for men to come drink and play poker.

Schumacher hired a decorator to create an authentic atmosphere in the room so that he could feel like a serious wine collector—if he ever started collecting.

Schumacher's father gave him the steel cigar door handles on the room's salvaged ash door.

Be Vawy, Vawy Quiet, I'm Hunting Wabbits

Most guys when they go hunting hope to bag a bird or two, maybe a deer if they're lucky. Shooting a 12-guage shotgun and feeling the short punch of the kickback on the shoulder brings pleasure enough. As does the bite of the chilly outdoors and the camaraderie that comes with tramping through forests and overgrown brush with a bunch of other guys.

Hubert Thummler has higher hopes. One day the 76-year-old businessman from Mexico aims to be the only man in the world to shoot all 46 of the world's sheep species. Right now he has 44 of them (only one other hunter has that many). This would put him well on his way to becoming known as one of history's most prolific hunters. As it stands, he has a good shot at that title, so to speak.

Currently, Thummler has traveled to all seven continents and bagged a grand total of 330 different animal species along the way. You name it, he has shot it, including lions, tigers, bears, elephants, alligators, and walruses.

Maybe even more amazing than Thummler's exploits are his trophies and his trophy house. All 330 specimens have been stuffed and mounted, some in their entirety, and positioned in the hunter's country home in the Mexican state of Querétaro. It's no surprise that he needs more space, though, so he is building a replica of a mountain inside an eight-story tower on his property that will hold most of his trophies. He plans to turn the space into a museum and donate it to the local town.

Apparently all of Thummler's hunting exploits are legal and done with the consent of local governments. And his adventures haven't escaped notice. Thummler has earned several international hunting awards as well as a certain amount of fame in hunting circles. And he's not done. There may be hooves, fur, and horns in every square inch of his house, but he won't be satisfied until he gets them all. Unless, of course, one gets him first.

Thummler poses with an altai argali, the world's largest sheep. Its horns can weigh up to 75 lb. The hunter traveled to Mongolia to find the animal in its native habitat.

A few gifts of tusks or antlers have been given to him by friends. Otherwise, all the animals in Hubert Thummler's house were shot by him.

Willis began looking for signed baseballs 30 years ago and keeps 20 of his favorites in a rack in his closet. He has personally collected signatures on over half of them.

ERNIE BANKS

A Cooperstown Closet

Sometimes men can claim entire buildings for their own space, whereas others are lucky to get a bedside table. Big or small, the rules of a man's territory are the same: Don't touch, it's mine. Retired real estate broker Trip Willis has spent his entire life collecting signed baseballs, player cards, and photographs of past ballplayers, but it wasn't until 1995 that he finally created a safe place to store and display his favorite stuff. That's when he and his wife built a house in Vermont with two walk-in closets: one for her and one for him. She filled hers with clothes. He turned his into a baseball vault of fame.

Willis hadn't always planned on storing his sports memorabilia in the closet. When he first moved into his house he kept many of his baseballs in the den. But with balls autographed by the likes of Joe DiMaggio and Mickey Mantle, Willis began to worry that someone could break in and take them. So he hid his favorites in the closet. The rest he put in a locked storage trunk in the attic.

These days, Willis's friends and family have caught the collecting bug and will call him when they run across a signed ball at a garage sale or auction. In fact, there's one ball he isn't finished with. Known as a "500 ball," it has been signed only by players who have hit 500 home runs in their careers, including Babe Ruth and Hank Aaron. All he's missing is signatures from a few of the newer guys who are still playing, like Barry Bonds and Sammy Sosa. Then he'll put it where only he can find it, right next to the ties.

Trip Willis's 5-ft. by 15-ft. walk-in closet does double duty as a very private display case for his baseball memorabilia.

Next to the caps and ties, Willis keeps a painting of his favorite player, Bobby Thompson of the former New York Giants, and a signed photo of Cincinnati Reds catcher Johnny Bench.

THREE

ENTERTAINI

"Some weasel took the cork out of my lunch." — *W.C. Fields*

If a manspace is created in the forest with no one around, does it really exist? For most of the guys in this chapter, the answer would be no. Some might say they're creating spaces for themselves, but most couldn't bear the thought of never showing their friends what a cool setup they have. Others make no secret of the fact that their manspaces exist for the sole purpose of entertaining friends.

Spaces made to entertain hold an important place in the realm of men-only rooms. They allow the owner to create his own atmosphere in his own way and they accommodate those less fortunate manspace-less men who have nowhere else to go to drink a cold beer or watch a good action movie with friends. Maine resident Jeff Johnson, who built an Irish beer pub and sports bar in his walk-out basement, has considered installing a neon "open" and "closed" sign to let friends know exactly when they can come over. John Morgan in Austin, Tex., simply opens the gate when he's in his backyard bar so friends can wander in if they're in the neighborhood.

PUTTING THE "FUN" BACK IN FUNCTIONAL

In addition to having a compelling atmosphere, these spaces need to be functional. Working beer taps, good ventilation, and comfortable seating are a few of the elements these men have to consider. In Andy Field's home theater he has to make sure the electronics work, the lights dim, and the seats rumble enough during the latest sci-fi epic. Dave McElroy created extra counter space and plenty of storage in his San Francisco kitchen to ensure he has enough prep room to cook for more people than just himself.

McElroy's kitchen is just one example of a manspace that serves nothing but the function of entertaining. After all, it's no fun and somewhat impractical to always cook for one. That's not to say that McElroy or any of the guys in this chapter don't enjoy their rooms when no one's around. They do, if only because they can keep tinkering with them. But if no one came around for a week or two, they might start feeling a little lost and lonely, and that usually means picking up the phone to invite everyone over on Friday night.

The round window in this typical saltbox garage is the only hint of what lies behind it. Otherwise, the manspace is completely camouflaged.

SAMURAI SPACE

All men think back fondly to the tea sets they had as boys, inviting friends over to eat make-believe crumpets and wafers. Just kidding. It was probably just the young boys with older sisters who got hoodwinked into putting down their MatchBox® cars and baseball mitts for a tea party. So why did a man in East Hampton, N.Y., turn a perfectly good garage into a Japanese tearoom and call it a manspace? Because he knows something most guys don't: Real men really do drink tea.

As a young man, the crisis-management specialist studied in Japan and developed a particular interest in

Traditional teahouse entrances were 2½-ft.-high doors that guests had to crawl through as a humbling gesture. Here, guests remove their shoes before climbing the narrow stairway.

16th-century Samurai warrior culture. As he tells it, these swordsmen not only studied the art of war but also created a tea ceremony and built teahouses in order to discuss the less-violent aspects of life, such as Zen Buddhism, philosophy, and art. Weapons were not allowed. Nor were women. For the Samurai, passing around a meditative cup of tea was as much a part of being a man as handling a sword.

Before creating his current space, the man carved out a serene corner of his apartment in New York City for tea and meditation. Eventually, though, his work as a crisis manager and communication expert got to be so stressful that he needed a more dedicated, peaceful place to wind down. That's when he and his wife bought the 10-acre weekend house in East Hampton and he turned the second floor of the garage into his tea room.

Everything about the manspace looks like a 16th-century teahouse, never mind its above-the-garage location. He asked Peter Wechsler, a craftsman trained in Japanese temple carpentry, to use traditionally rustic materials in the room, such as imported clay and straw stucco for the walls and peeled reed and bamboo for the ceiling. Wechsler also used traditional building techniques when possible. Instead of using nails, he scribed

In traditional Japanese teahouses, room size is linked to tatami mat size—this is a four tatami space. The round window is a reference to the Zen notion of yin and yang.

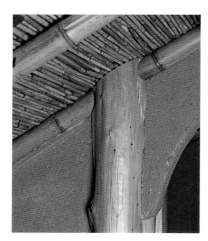

Carpenter Peter Wechsler scribed and hand-carved all the joints in the room, including the junction of this eastern red cedar post and a bamboo ceiling joist.

The scroll in the *tokanoma* or alcove is an 18th-century original made by a famous Japanese monk. The polished Japanese plateau stone represents both stability and the passing of time.

and hand-carved the joinery. Also, the simple room has no furniture—guests remove their shoes at the entrance, then sit on bamboo mats on the floor like the Samurai would have done. There's an authentic 16th-century Samurai sword symbolically left on a low display counter at the top of the stairs to remind guests that, before entering, the exterior world must be left behind. Though no one has yet unpacked a revolver, talk of politics inside the tearoom is prohibited.

Instead the talk is of art. Another authentic element to the teahouse is the *tokanoma*, an altar-like alcove built into the room to display Buddhist scrolls and other symbolic artwork. The Samurai changed the art in the *tokanoma* at least each season, so the owner, who has an extensive collection of Asian art and unique Japanese rocks, rotates the objects when the mood strikes him.

The only time this guy drinks tea is during a ceremony (the rest of the time he's a coffee drinker). And because it's not appropriate to have a tea ceremony alone, he often heads up to the tearoom just for meditation. Like the men who started the teahouse tradition, he relishes the chance to leave the real world battles behind.

HOW STUFF WORKS
THE TEA CEREMONY

The Japanese tea ceremony has a long history, starting with the Samurai, who would drink tea before battle to calm the mind. Buddhist monks in the 16th century were also fond of tea because it kept them awake for rigorous meditation lasting up to 20 hours a day. Japanese tea is different from western tea—the leaves are not roasted but dried and then ground into a powder. Dissolved in hot water, the tea is a bitter, highly caffeinated drink. In a tea ceremony, a single bowl is passed communally around the room. Afterward, the bowl is washed with fresh cold water as a final show of respect to the guests.

Lights automatically come on
when the doors to the electron-

MR. GADGET

When Andy Field's wife Rose refers to his high-tech home theater as "Man Land," it's not because he watches sci-fi movies or drinks beer in there (even though he does). It's because he has a stack of electronic toys and computerized controls that most men would drool over. Aside from the cable box, amplifier, DVD player, and X-Box® video game system he has for the 65-in. television, Field, who is a retired Microsoft® programmer, can control music and lights throughout the entire house from a touch-pad computer screen installed in one wall. He also wired in a collection of transducers—disk-shaped low-frequency subwoofers—and attached them to the theater's couches and floor so that the room vibrates during explosions, rocket blastoffs, or alien landings. The special effects coup de grâce, however, is that there isn't a wire, speaker, or LED light visible in the entire theater.

With the fridge and the electronics hidden behind Andy Field's wood cabinets, the movie is the center of attention in "Man Land."

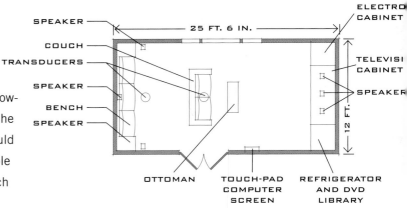

Before Field claimed the space it was a dark, below-ground bedroom in the 1962 split-level ranch house he and his wife own in Seattle. He always thought it would make a good media room but it wasn't until the couple decided to remodel the entire house that his high-tech dreams became real.

READY TO RUMBLE

The architects on the job, Julie Campbell and Buzz Tenenbom, were told to brighten up the house. They added windows and doors and removed interior walls.

Simple wood finishes imbue the place with a natural but clean look. Field wanted the same theme in the home theater. He also wanted the architects to hide the electronic equipment and wires so that the only thing visible at movie time was the TV screen.

Field has several hundred DVDs that he keeps behind a cabinet next to the television (that's also where the refrigerator is). In addition to his science fiction flicks, like *Lord of the Rings* and *The Matrix,* he keeps classics like *Citizen Kane* on hand as well as a growing collection of Disney movies for his three-year-old daughter. The small theater can hold five people comfortably on two couches, and when it's not family movie night (which it is often), Field rounds up his guy friends to come watch a good action movie. The opening launch scene in *Apollo 13* can make the room rumble like it's heading to the moon.

Every detail was considered in creating this entertainment Shangri-La. Refrigerator drawers slide out for easy access to beer and wine just below Andy Field's DVD collection.

Comedy and tragedy masks that Field found online hang on the wall panels beneath two tiny black speakers. Lights in the room are programmed to dim slowly as the movie starts.

Honey, I'll Be in the Sports Bar

Sports and beer often mix. Beer and the living room carpet do not. Neither, for that matter, do sports and family members who want to watch *Thomas the Tank Engine* DVDs on the only television in the house. That's why many men find freedom at their local sports bar. The game is always on and no one's going to mind if a few suds hit the floor after the winning touchdown.

Jeff Johnson has had his fair share of both sports and bars. He was the starting running back for Cornell University in the mid-1980s and made the all-Ivy League first team in his senior season. Of course, having grown up outside Toronto, hockey is a big part of his life too. He plays forward for a men's league in Portland, Maine. For 15 years he and his wife moved from city to city with his job as a marketing specialist for a waste management company. During that time, he visited plenty of bars in Atlanta, Houston, Charlotte, and elsewhere trying to catch the big game. But what he really wanted was an entertainment room at home. He just never wanted to build one, as he knew he'd be packing up and moving on to the next town a year or two later.

Then, in 2001, Johnson stopped traveling and he and his wife and their two young daughters moved to Maine. There they bought a three-bedroom house with a walk-out basement that was perfect for the sports bar Jeff had been imagining for years.

The natural-gas fireplace was installed by the manufacturer and stone masons built the façade and the mantel so Johnson could have a place to display mementos from his travels.

No, this is not a neighborhood pub in London. It's Jeff Johnson's basement in Maine that he outfitted with stained maple, birch, and pine to look like an English local.

BELLYING UP

The very next fall, Johnson began sketching out designs for the empty basement. In one corner he planned a media room with a big-screen TV to watch games. Outside, under a deck overhang, he wanted a hot tub for extended halftime breaks. The rest of the space was devoted to a wine cellar and the main bar.

The atmosphere of the space was influenced by the various watering holes Johnson had visited over the years. A "C"-shaped wood-paneled bar, leather-topped stools, and a stone-clad fireplace are all features from his favorite English and Irish pubs. Growing up, Johnson had helped his father, a carpenter, with woodworking projects, so he felt confident doing the framing and the paneling himself. He hired professional tradesmen to install the fireplace and the electricity.

After three long years working mostly during the winters, Johnson finished the bar. After stocking it with couches and bar tables, he framed his college football mementos and hockey keepsakes and hung them around the room. Then he brought in the televisions—one behind the bar, one in the media room, and one hanging from the ceiling in one corner. Anyone over for the game would be hard pressed to miss a play, no matter where they are sitting.

Now Johnson invites friends over for Sunday afternoon games. For the big ones, like the Super Bowl or the World Series, as many as 50 people show up. Even when there isn't a game on, neighbors and Johnson's fellow hockey players come over for cocktails, sometimes unannounced. Some friends have even suggested that Johnson get a neon "open" and "closed" sign—just like any good sports bar.

Johnson's bar is a great place to drink and watch sports, but it's also a repository for footballs and other mementos from his glory days on the Cornell gridiron.

To make sure no one misses part of the game while soaking in the bar's outdoor hot tub, built just under a first-floor deck, Johnson installed a TV that swivels to face out the window.

When the bar is closed John-son's kids have movie nights on the big screen. At the height of football season, though, it's all sports in high definition.

During the kitchen renovation McElroy replaced an old Wedgewood stove with a Garland®. Even the 24-in.-wide Northland fridge is sized to get the most use out of the small space.

SMALL KITCHEN, BIG FOOD

Men usually take whatever space they can get, no matter how small. But if you're planning to cook elaborate meals for a big group of friends, which food lover David McElroy does often, you'll need some room. Unfortunately, that's just what was missing from McElroy's 1,100-sq.-ft. apartment in San Francisco's Mission district when he bought the place five years ago. The kitchen itself was a tiny 8-ft. by 10-ft. room. There was no drawer space. A giant pantry took up too much space. (McElroy installed a metal shelving unit and closed the door.) The small tile countertops were not only chipped and impossible to keep clean, but they were too shallow and difficult to get to because the overhead cabinetry was too low.

So like many guys, McElroy set out to fix up the space to meet his needs. He called an artist friend, Bo Williams, who was just getting started in the cabinetry business and could give McElroy a good deal on the remodel. McElroy, who craves order when he cooks, wanted to turn the tiny room into an efficient workspace where any tool he needed was within easy reach.

The deep stainless-steel sink is surrounded by the concrete countertop, which McElroy chose for its cool gray color and easy cleanup.

An 8-ft.-long countertop and a bank of cabinets and shelves replaced an oversized pantry, offering plenty of prep space.

MAKING ROOM

The first thing Williams did was remove the oversize pantry and replace it with an 8-ft.-long countertop. Above that he put a bank of cabinets and open shelves. The old tile was ripped out along with the cabinets. Concrete was poured for the countertops. McElroy then agreed on a bamboo veneer for the face frames and cabinet doors. Last, to give the room a larger appearance Williams widened the doorway to the kitchen so that McElroy could talk to people in the dining room as he cooked.

As the construction took shape, Williams began incorporating some ingenious storage features, like a chest-high bank of deep drawers that extends from the ground up to the top cabinets and a pull-out cutting board that hides behind a row of fake drawers. In one corner of dead space next to the dishwasher he crafted a set of slide-out racks for McElroy's stock pots. Even the extra deep stainless-steel sink doubles as a workspace with the addition of a grated steel rack. Now McElroy has everything he needs within arm's reach and enough space to cook for at least eight. Cleanup is easy too, even for friends who end up doing the dishes while he sips his after-dinner cappuccino.

A chest-high bank of bamboo-veneer drawers and open shelving gives McElroy plenty of storage and quick access to ingredients, dishes, and utensils.

The Manhouse

For some men, getting a space for themselves requires quick thinking. When John Morgan and his wife Natasha bought their two-bedroom bungalow in Austin, Tex., in October 2000, they had never seen the inside of the carriage house in the backyard. As the previous owner's storage shed, the space had been so stuffed with junk that the doors wouldn't open and the windows were too dirty to see through. Their realtor told them that it had been built by a cabinetmaker in the late 1970s as a workshop to restore old pianos and that it was wired and had a bathroom. Because the

house was too good to pass up, the Morgans signed the mortgage papers never having seen the inside of the carriage house.

After the closing, Morgan and a friend decided to find out just what shape the mystery space was in. As the building was filled to the rafters with trash, old appliances, and unsalvageable furniture, they struggled to get the doors open. Slowly they were able to gain inches by reaching inside and pulling out whatever they could touch. As Morgan and his friend got farther inside the 200-sq.-ft. building and the space began to clear, Morgan realized he had something special. "I felt like an archeologist discovering an old pyramid," he says. The lights were burned out but he could see that the interior, though only a basic frame, was constructed by a professional. On both sides of the roof, two dormers with operable casement windows (that matched

John Morgan stands in front of his backyard "Manhouse," where friends come to drink and drop off paraphernalia banned from their own homes.

The actual bar inside the space came from a friend who worked in the movie business. It was a prop in the John Travolta movie *Michael*, part of which was shot in Austin.

No manspace would be complete without a cardboard cutout of Elvis, concert posters, and a leg lamp, which Morgan calls "the electric sex at the end of the bar" in homage to the movie *A Christmas Story.*

the ones in the end gable), had been installed to add natural light. Plus, there were electrical outlets fastened to the studs nearly every 3 ft.

FINDERS KEEPERS

Morgan knew he had to move fast so his wife wouldn't come up with any ideas of her own about how to use the space. Once the carriage house was cleared, he quietly put a bar in the corner of the room and plugged in a small refrigerator behind it. Later, he managed to add a dart-board, some Christmas lights, and a few other odds and ends before Natasha realized something was going on. She confronted Morgan, saying, "What do you think this is, a manhouse?" The name stuck.

In a few months, the place was filled with neon signs, ashtrays, beer cans, and music posters for local bands, and the couple had worked out a détente. Filling the space with furniture from garage sales, they began doing most of their

entertaining in the Manhouse. Natasha's brothers spend time out there playing cards. Her father enjoys having a place to smoke his cigars.

As word of the backyard bar spread among the Morgans' group of friends, people began donating every-thing from old radios to mannequins. Now the Morgans have a three-year-old son, Luke, and the bar has turned into something of a toy store. "You can't break anything in there," says Morgan. But rarely a weekend night goes by where Morgan and a few buddies don't have a beer and play pinball or darts. It is, after all, his space.

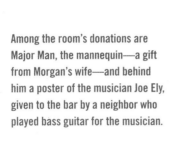

Among the room's donations are Major Man, the mannequin—a gift from Morgan's wife—and behind him a poster of the musician Joe Ely, given to the bar by a neighbor who played bass guitar for the musician.

Whereas some guys need a manspace, others need outer space. Such is the case with Internet technician Gary Reighn, who has transformed his Philadelphia basement into a home theatre called "The Bridge," an elaborate replica of the USS Enterprise's main control room. Though he did watch the original *Star Trek* growing up, Reighn doesn't think of himself as a Trekkie. Or at least that's what he says. According to Reighn, the main reason for the renovation was to give his large electronics collection a home. The *Star Trek* theme was a way to have fun and create something unique. Most would agree he's accomplished his feat.

Using an amateur's collection of power tools and know-how, Reighn framed out a room in half of his empty basement and wired it to hold a projector with a DVD player and 100-in. screen, complete with surround-sound speakers. Then he detailed the room with back-lit *Star Trek* insignia, "viewports" showing illuminated star fields, fake computer screens, and a pocket door to imitate the automatic entrance of the real spaceship, sans the hydraulic sound effect.

Now Reighn and his son watch TV and movies or play video games in the basement theater almost every night. Reighn's wife is happy with the arrangement, too. The entertainment center and speakers are now permanently out of the living room. Kirk and the crew couldn't have done better.

If You Build It, They Will Come . . . to Eat

The way Jim Richmond tells it, the best thing about the remote Vermont cabin (and its 1950s-style kitchen) he built is the friends that like to stay for the weekend and prepare nice dinners in it. "I myself am not a good cook," he says. His friends, however, are. And after living and working in New York City for 40 years as a portrait artist and building contractor in SoHo, he seems to have quite a few such friends. Chefs from New York's Raoul's restaurant, Brooklyn's Long Tan Thai restaurant, and a California Ritz Carlton have all cranked up Richmond's 80-year-old gas-burning stove with delicious results. In years past he has even had the pleasure of eating dinners prepared by René Verdon, the Kennedy White House chef.

When Richmond isn't entertaining—or rather when he isn't letting others entertain in his space—he still starts and ends his days in the kitchen, cooking all his own meals and eating them at the one-person table next to the tin cabinet sink. During the long winters the snow is too deep for visitors and Richmond spends months at a time with only his paintings and his horses, which he breeds and trains for harness races. It's the kind of lifestyle he imagined when he first moved to the Green Mountain State 15 years ago. That's when he first started building the cabin he lives in now (as well as a horse barn, painting studio, and equipment shed).

Because he wanted the house to be cozy and inviting, he built it himself in the style of a bungalow, searching through magazines for examples and paying attention to the smallest details. The kitchen has 16-in. crown molding, floor-to-ceiling paneling, and a salvaged door from the property's original farmhouse, lending the room a warm, Craftsman-like quality. Aside from the 1920s Glenwood® stove, which a friend had kept in Richmond's barn for nearly a decade before deciding

Richmond's 1920s gas-burning Glenwood stove has three ovens and a plate warmer. Its original cream and pale green colors were matched for the walls, trim, and cabinets in the rest of the kitchen.

A tiny kitchen table and tin sink cabinet represent Richmond's uncluttered style—and lack of counter space. Instead of electric lights, Richmond uses candles and kerosene lamps like the one on the table to cook by.

Richmond's cowboy hat and horse harnesses hang on a door salvaged from the property's original farmhouse. The blue glass in the upper cabinet doors adds another masculine touch to the room.

The Fiestaware pitcher on the shelf above the sink and Richmond's other kitchen furnishings were all found at a local flea market. The corner cabinet was salvaged from a friend's teardown and painted to match the stove.

he didn't want it anymore, the furnishings are classically 1950s. Cast-iron skillets, ceramic Fiestaware®, and tin teapots—all of which Richmond found at local flea markets for less than $5 each—add to the throwback feel.

Another detail about Richmond's cabin is that there's no electricity. Candles come in handy for more than good atmosphere at dinner. In the winter, the Glenwood stove does double duty as oven and heater. In January, when he's at home alone, Richmond tends to keep his coat on a little longer, but in December, when guests arrive for the holidays and start to fill up the kitchen, the house is as warm as ever.

GEAR
STILL COOKING AFTER ALL THESE YEARS

Jim Richmond's friend kept his 1928 Glenwood gas range in Richmond's barn for ten years with its face to the wall before giving it to Richmond. It was only then that Richmond got his first look at it. The Glenwood brand first started appearing in the late 19th century as a wood-burning model and quickly became a stalwart of the industry. By the early 1920s the company had started making gas ranges and some smaller models for apartment dwellers. Richmond's stove has six burners, two ovens, a broiler, and a warming oven—plenty of space to cook for a house-load of friends.

BACHELOR PAD PARADISE

Bachelors have plenty of space to claim for themselves. How they claim it is another matter. After Los Angeles resident Dale Sizer visited Hawaii one year, he came home and decided he wasn't ready to give up his tropical vacation so readily. So he bought some bamboo wallpaper and plastered it onto the white living room walls in his West Hollywood apartment. Inspired, he began to transform the entire 850-sq.-ft. two-bedroom place into a tiki pad worthy of a set from the movie *South Pacific*.

Sizer, who is a painter and computer graphic illustrator, began shopping swap meets and flea markets looking for anything with a tropical character. He bought wooden masks and paintings of topless island beauty queens. Zebra-skin carpet was installed throughout the house, and a rattan bar was put in place in the living room. He also had a C-shaped couch built and upholstered it with a reptile-skin cover. Nothing was left untouched by the tropical makeover. His bedroom featured palm fronds and a conga drum to give it that "jungle hut vibe." He even upholstered his television sets in animal-skin fabrics.

After more than ten years in the apartment, Sizer no longer collects tiki gear. Instead, he spends his spare time working on his cars, a custom hot rod and a 1961 Dodge that he's outfitting with glitter carpet and an oblong steering wheel. That doesn't mean he's getting tired of his pad—he still loves watching the reaction first-time visitors have when they come over. It's just that his tastes are veering more toward the road these days than the beach.

Before transforming his apartment into a tiki paradise, Dale Sizer built a loft-size painting studio over the living room, creating a ceiling in the shape of an artist's palette.

As every bachelor longs to do, Sizer created a jungle theme in the bedroom, with bamboo wallpaper, zebra-skin carpet, a leopard bedspread, and a drum light surrounded by dried palm leaves.

After upholstering the dashboard of one of his cars with animal-skin fabric, Sizer wrapped his television sets so they too would fit in with the overall groovy tiki vibe.

F O U R

PLAYING

"We don't stop playing because we get old, we get old because we stop playing." — *George Bernard Shaw*

Most men consider the idea of building a space to play in as instinctive as standing up to relieve themselves. As boys we built forts and hideouts with everything from sheets to cardboard boxes. Vacant lots in the neighborhood would play host to pick-up baseball games as long as there was room enough to create an infield with a few tires, rocks, or balled-up T-shirts. These childhood spaces came about naturally. Besides that, we were encouraged to make them by the people we lived with (namely, our parents). So why should that be different now?

Needing to play is no different for men than it is for boys. And let's not forget that an important part of playing is the toys we have to play with—a space alone does not fun make. What's changed from boyhood is what we play with and where we play our games. Sheets and cardboard have become renovated barns and refinished basements. Nerf balls and sixth-grade science kits have become golf clubs and deep space telescopes. Granted, men's play spaces and their toys cost more, but part of the fun is going out and buying a bunch of new gear anyway, whether it's a closet full of electronics, a new pool cue, or a six pack of fine English ale.

How men play has also changed from when we were boys, though in some instances, not so much. We still like to play games, only now instead of tiddlywinks it's Texas hold'em. Cars are still fun too, though we prefer to drive them these days rather than push them around on the floor. In Vermont, a mechanical engineer still plays with his toy trains, only now they're bigger and more expensive and he no longer has friends who come over and try to smash up his set. Other men have taken on adult-only games. Four friends in Connecticut who call themselves the Wine Boys rented out a place of their own to not only drink a good glass of vino but to make it as well.

The manspaces in this chapter provide proof that the play we had in us as boys is alive and well in us as men. That's why they were all built with good fun in mind. They house everything from poker tables to recording equipment to outdoor fire pits, and in them men can drink, play music, and gamble—not quite the games they played as boys, but games nonetheless.

It's never too early for a glass of vino at the Wine Boys winery, where (from left) Richard Gibbons, Bob Benoit, Tony Izzo, and Coz Filiberto enjoy a breakfast of donuts and Cabernet Sauvignon.

The Wine Boys still keep the grape press Izzo's uncle brought over from Italy decades ago.

THE WINE BOYS

It all started innocently enough in Tony Izzo's Connecticut basement in 1973. He and his uncle, who had brought over the family wine recipe from Italy, would crush and press grapes until they had about 10 gallons of juice. Then they'd let it ferment in plastic and glass containers and hope for the best. Each year they'd get about three cases of drinkable but strong red wine. Carrying on the family tradition was fun, says Izzo, but drinking what they made was not great, at least not until the second or third glass.

Any time is the right time for a glass of red for the Wine Boys, especially during strategy meetings in the winery.

When Izzo took over the wine-making chores by himself, he began to investigate ways to make better wine. About that time his friend, Richard Gibbons, started helping out. Not long after that the two were joined by Bob Benoit and Coz Filiberto. The four friends figured that better wine started with better grapes, so they bought batches of Cabernet Sauvignon grapes imported from California. In a few years, they were getting more and more compliments from friends and family and everyone was having a great time—there was at least as much wine drinking as there was making. The problem was that Izzo's basement was getting too small for the operation (they were using 2,000 lb. of grapes to make about 140 gal. of wine a year). With the increased production, fruit flies and a constant smell of alcohol were inundating Izzo's house, which wasn't pleasing his wife in the least.

So in 2003 the four friends decided to leave the basement and start an official wine-making business. They

Tony Izzo watches as the bottle machine automatically lifts a bottle into a fitting where it pushes open a valve to let the wine flow in. Once the bottle is filled, the machine lowers it and the flow stops.

Bob Benoit applies a label by hand for the 2004 vintage. Recently, the Wine Boys sprang for a bottle-labeling machine that also automatically corks.

Richard Gibbons refills an oak barrel after cleaning it out. The wine is aged as long as a year in these containers, but it is temporarily removed while the barrels are cleaned every three months.

rented a 2,000-sq.-ft. warehouse space inside an old rubber extrusion plant in Bridgeport, calling their operation The Wine Boys LLC. After a few toasts to their new venture, they spent six months taking out walls, installing floor tile, and painting. The next step was to buy gear. Instead of fermenting and aging wine in plastic and glass, the guys bought a 3,000-liter stainless steel tank and oak barrels. They also got a professional bottling machine that fills about 800 bottles an hour.

These days the wine boys process about 18,000 lb. of grapes each year in two stainless-steel tanks. They've labeled their wine (still mostly Cabernet Sauvignon) Black Rock Vintners after Bridgeport's Black Rock Harbor and sell mostly to local restaurants, package stores, and private buyers. The busiest times at the winery are in the fall, just after the grapes are harvested, and in the spring, when the finished wine is bottled. Because all the guys have professional jobs in addition to being grape crushers—Izzo is a real estate broker, Gibbons is an attorney, Benoit is a banker, and Filiberto is a doctor—they take shifts at the winery to do everything from cleaning out the barrels to labeling new bottles. All four also manage to get together at the winery at least once a month for meetings, meals, and wine tastings. As always, keeping a careful eye on quality is everyone's favorite job.

⛹ VICTORY LAP
THE WINE BOYS UNCORKED

In the wine business the date or vintage on a bottle refers to the year in which the grapes were harvested. Because the Wine Boys just got off the ground, their first commercially available wine was the 2004 vintage, though they did have a 2003 Cabernet Sauvignon available for tasting. The first sip of the wine has a bite to it. After ten minutes, though, it mellows into a robust cherry and earthy flavor with hints of licorice and vanilla, no doubt from the French and American oak barrels where it ages. The full-bodied taste lingers on the tongue long after it goes down, making this a smooth bottle of red.

IN HIS ROOM

Before Mark Blaha got his own space, he put his recording studio in one half of a renovated old barn on his spread 30 minutes outside Philadelphia while his wife Georgette set up her weaving studio in the other half. It didn't take long for them to realize that loud music and textiles don't go together.

Lucky for him, the couple needed extra space to store tractors and mowers, so he hired architect Peter Archer to design a new barn with room for a studio. The 900-sq.-ft. space has a main music room, a small mixing station, a kitchenette, a loft room, and a bathroom. Mark chose an all-wood interior because it helps absorb sound better than wallboard or concrete. Exposed trusses in the vaulted ceiling also help break up the music.

Blaha, who toured with rock bands through the 1980s and 1990s, spends time every day in the studio. After years crammed into a tour bus with other musicians, he enjoys the open space and solitude of the barn. There's a bass setup, drums, three electric and three acoustic guitars, and an electric mandolin. He and his blues band practice regularly in the music room and his teenage son, who goes to boarding school nearby, comes over to jam with his dad on weekends. On occasion, Blaha, who is retired, rents the space to local bands as a favor. In his control room he mixes and records songs with a professional collection of electronics. For Blaha, having his own space to do what he wants whenever he wants is the best tune he's come up with yet.

GEAR
READY TO RECORD

If you're planning a recording studio of your own, there's no sense in skimping on electronics. Mark Blaha uses a 24-track mixing board aided by effects units and a compressor/limiter to monitor volume and alter the sound. For digital recordings, he uses an 8-track digital recorder or a laptop with Performer® software. Songs can be transferred to CD on one of two CD recorders or to cassette through a dual cassette recorder, and the playback is through midsize Alesis® Monitor 2 speakers. In the music room he keeps Electro-Voice® speakers as well as Electro-Voice monitors and a Crown® power amp— reason enough to stop playing music, kick back on the couch, and have a good listen.

Blaha cuts all the grass on his 20-acre farm himself, so he built a barn for tractors, riding mowers, and his recording studio.

Blaha plays the drums while two friends rock out on guitar inside the barn. The Persian carpets and metal chandelier help cut down on the amount of reverb in the room.

LET THE GAMES BEGIN

Maine resident Dan Cunliffe II likes his games. After he and his wife Angie were married in 1992 they built a house, and before the carpet was down he'd moved a Ping-Pong® table into the empty basement. That was when Cunliffe let Angie know that she could decorate the rest of the house however she wanted. The bottom floor was his.

Cunliffe always wanted a place he could hang out with his guy friends and store his vast collection of autographed sports memorabilia and celebrity photographs. Before he met Angie, he'd been living with his parents, sleeping in his boyhood bedroom, and his options were limited. When he decided to build his own place he made sure to include a roomy basement.

After a couple of years with just the Ping-Pong table to amuse him, Cunliffe made the move to create a full-blown manspace. He laid down carpet, trimmed windows, installed a dropped-tile ceiling, and painted the walls.

Signed celebrity photographs line the walls next to a championship blanket, a life-size cardboard cutout of Red Sox pitcher Curt Schilling, and a video poker machine Cunliffe's mother-in-law donated to the game room.

Dan Cunliffe's Auburn, Maine, game-room basement measures 1,100 sq. ft. and includes a pool table, video games, pinball machines, and signed sports memorabilia.

Then he brought in extra toys. First was a standard-size pool table and a television to watch baseball and football games. Later, he added a full-size Pac-Man® video game, circa 1981, and two pinball machines. The crowning touch was a video poker game his mother-in-law gave him.

PAC-MAN FEVER

For most folks, locating vintage Pac-Man video games or pinball machines would be a tough chore. Cunliffe was able to get them through the business that he and his dad own, which specializes in collectibles. The store has also

Cunliffe's collection is mostly sentimental, though it does have real value, including a signed Babe Ruth postcard worth about $3,000. Hanging at right is Cunliffe's World Series ticket from 2004.

A Pac-Man game and two pinball machines from the 1980s sit next to a framed and signed Boston Red Sox jersey from Cunliffe's favorite player, Johnny Damon.

provided a source for Cunliffe's impressive collection of sports memorabilia and celebrity autographs. The man is a lifelong Red Sox and Patriots fan and has oodles of stuff related to those two teams. In fact, the lion's share of decoration in the basement game room consists of baseballs, jerseys, caps, and posters of Cunliffe's sports heroes. The rest of the walls and shelves are covered with autographed headshots of famous people like Bob Hope. Hey, it's his manspace. He can do what he wants.

When Cunliffe's buddies come over it's usually for a game, but unless it's fourth down on the one yard line with one minute left, hardly anyone just watches TV. Cunliffe and his friends shoot pool or try to get lucky on the poker machine. Though the room is his and all his, Cunliffe and his wife will occasionally host parties there together. Their nine-year-old son has his end-of-the-season little league parties there because the team loves to play pinball (the coaches like the pool table). Also, Cunliffe has set up some exercise equipment, which he can use while watching television. With all the games around, he has to keep in shape somehow.

VICTORY LAP
AUTOGRAPH MAN

Dan Cunliffe's memorabilia ranges from the sentimental (a framed local newspaper declaring the Red Sox victory in the World Series) to the valuable (a signed Babe Ruth postcard worth about $3,000) to the truly corny (a photograph of Cunliffe with Baywatch actress Stacy Kamano). His list of face-to-face meetings with sports and film celebrities is over 30 names long and he has the photographs to prove it. Every snapshot is framed and hung up around the basement, which has become as much a showroom for Cunliffe's stuff as it is a place to blow off some steam with a little pinball.

TRAIN'S A-COMIN'

Young boys love trains, especially the old-fashioned steam engines with hulking black tanks, the proud smokestacks, and the churning wheels rumbling down the track. When Randy Arnold was a boy he had an electric train set that his father had set up in their small New York City apartment atop several dressers. To have enough room for the track layout, his dad built wooden trestles between the dressers that would fold down when not in use.

As he got older, his passion for trains only grew. When he had a son of his own, Arnold got into toy trains with his boy. Then the family moved and the train set was packed away. In 2001, Arnold and his wife bought a new house. While moving in, Arnold, who is a mechanical engineer, ran across his son's train set and decided to set it up for himself. There was a spare room in the basement, so he built a platform and installed an oval track around the room.

Arnold favors brass replicas of trains from the 1940s and early 1950s. Currently he's building and painting 12 freight cars as part of a fictional production line.

Arnold's train set comes through a hole in the hallway and into the furnace room. The metal rods with red balls are manual controls for switching trains onto various tracks.

Before poking a hole in the wall and extending his tracks, Arnold had an oval in this tiny basement room. For reference, he uses magazine clips and photos of trains he's visited.

Before long, Arnold began hanging out with fellow enthusiasts in the neighborhood, trying out engines and cars and virgin stretches of track. It wasn't long before train envy got the better of him and he decided it was time to improve upon his simple oval. "The other guys had layouts that were point to point rather than round, and the trains could switch to multiple tracks," he says. So he went back home and sawed a hole through one wall in the workshop to an adjoining hallway. Then he built a platform along the wall of the hallway and into the home's furnace room. This would give him both a small tunnel and room enough to allow his trains to switch onto several other tracks.

There are some weekends that Arnold doesn't come out of the basement. In addition to piecing together and painting the various buildings, he builds and paints all his train cars by hand, wiring new engines with a collection of gear that includes a set of old dental tools. Arnold's trains may only travel from one room to the next, but the fun he's had over the years has taken him a long way from his boyhood setup atop the dressers in his family's New York apartment.

To build model trains, Arnold has to wear magnifying glasses and use tools small enough to exact the tiniest detail.

Mills hinged old doors to trees along a pathway in his garden and labeled them door numbers 1, 2, and 3 as a tip of the hat to *Alice in Wonderland*.

OUT OF SERVICE

THE GREAT OUTDOORS

The need for manspace sometimes draws men into flights of fancy that four walls and a roof cannot contain. And who can blame them? When acquiring a space of their own after years spent tiptoeing among someone else's things, lots of men start imagining the endless possibilities of what they can do. Landscape designer Ken Mills saw a flat field behind his Vermont house and imagined a stage.

Mills wasn't faced with the challenge of finding room for himself inside the house. His challenge was finding room outside. Before he bought his 18th-century cabin and the two wooded acres behind it, he rented apartments in New York and small houses in Burlington. Because they never belonged to him, he never wanted to spend the money to fix them up. Even after he bought his current place he wasn't happy. He had land—that was a great start—but it didn't have the trees, meandering brooks,

and privacy he always wanted. Still, the price on the house was too good to pass up, so he bought it, rolled up his sleeves, and started digging.

PATHS TO NOWHERE

As a landscape designer, Mills is used to transforming plain yards into something special. He is, however, having trouble convincing his clients to let him do to their land what he has done to his. Before getting into landscaping, Mills was involved in theater production and set construction, so when it came time to landscape his own yard he decided to blend his current profession with his old one. In ten years he has transformed the once flat backyard into a collection of whimsical outdoor rooms that have more in common with installation art or stage sets than landscaped gardens. Concrete mushrooms sprout along meandering pathways. A half-buried soda machine tempts visitors to peer around the next corner. Salvaged doors hinged to trees lead to nowhere. A Celtic stone labyrinth invites wandering souls into its magical maze.

True to his theatrical roots, Mills hosts performances in his gardens. Audiences wander among the garden pathways and through the various "rooms," encountering

dancers, musicians, and poets. Impromptu bands strike up some tunes around the fire pit.

Of course, Mills also enjoys his gardens alone. On summer mornings he reads the newspapers and eats breakfast on a stone patio next to a waterfall emptying into a fish-stocked pond. Where there was once nothing but grass, there are now lush landscapes. The yard has turned out to be Mills's best set design yet.

Ken Mills hangs out in his fire pit "room" with buddies Michael Cassidy and Brian Yarwood (with banjo).

Mills sits in what used to be a flat yard of dirt behind his house.

Mills hauled in stones to create this traditional Celtic labyrinth. Guests take a meditative walk along the pathway to where Mills installed "the throne"—two inverted cedar roots holding a glass ball.

DOOR IN THE FLOOR

Men find room for their hobbies in the darnedest places. Take Eric Deam. His tiny house in the Berkeley Hills was built on top of a concrete cistern that stored water for the local fire department in the 1940s. When Eric bought the place the 22-ft.-deep round tank was dark and dank and only accessible by a trapdoor in the living room. At first, Eric briefly flirted with the idea of filling the cistern with water and having indoor pool parties. Local building codes put the kibosh on that one. He then realized that if he couldn't have a pool to play in, he could turn the tank into a music room and home recording studio.

Eric, who works as a computer engineer, almost missed the opportunity to buy the 675-sq.-ft. home (825 sq. ft. with the cistern). He found the place on the very same day he put an offer down on another house. Deam had been feeling ambivalent about the offer, so he took a drive and ran across an open-house sign in front of the bungalow with the cistern. He was immediately intrigued by its location. The place sits on a hillside and is accessible only by walking up about 100 steps. As far as Eric was concerned, that bit of inconvenience paid off when saw the views of Berkeley and San Francisco Bay. Though the inside was "a box with two walls and four small compartments," Eric bought it. He then called his brother, designer Chris Deam, and an architect friend from college, Thom Faulders, to come renovate the midcentury cabin from top to cistern.

Before Deam's 1951 cabin was renovated, the front door was on the other side of the house and opened into the mechanical room. Now the first thing guests see is a view of Berkeley and the East Bay.

Deam's cabin sits atop two metal beams attached to the top of a cistern that's 14 ft. in diameter. The hard plastic railings around the cistern entrance match the colored plastic cabinets in the kitchen.

After a long struggle trying to decide the best material for the cistern's entrance railings, Deam and his architects decided on perforated clear Plexiglas to preserve the view and the modern aesthetic of the house.

So that the ladder leading into the music room wouldn't be too steep, Deam's architects staggered the descent with a landing and steps that were anchored to the concrete wall and suspended from the ceiling.

Like most guys with dedicated spaces, Deam gets serious with his hobby and his equipment, like this microphone and voice filter.

CISTERN CHALET

Eric gave the architects three guidelines: Maximize the view, add storage, and make the cistern part of the house. Chris and Thom took out two walls and added several windows and a glass door to bring the view into sharp focus. Most of the cistern is underground, except for a section under the home's front deck that provided just enough room to add a small window. The designers also covered the original trapdoor with Plexiglas® so that light coming in from above would shine into the cistern. That made getting into the music room the project's biggest challenge. Eric didn't want a staircase that started on one side of the house and ended on the far side of the cistern—there just wasn't enough room. He also didn't want a treacherous 22-ft. ladder. So Chris and Thom came up

with a unique ladder-and-stair combination in which they suspended the lower steps from the ceiling with steel rods.

The cistern now doubles as Eric's recording studio and home office. Having studied music at the California Polytechnic Institute, he tries to keep up with his classical guitar background. Rock and experimental pop is where the fun is for him though, so he spends most of his time with the volume and distortion turned up. One of the built-in benefits of having a cistern as a music room is that it's underground and totally soundproof, so he doesn't have to worry about bugging the neighbors. In Deam's music room it's as loud as he wants it to be.

Wood beams are visible behind the original concrete walls in Eric Deam's cistern-turned-recording studio. He's set up for digital recording and can engineer songs straight to CD or through his computer.

For aspiring recording artists without cisterns under their houses, one way to keep the sound more to yourself is to make existing walls soundproof. When sound waves hit a standard stud-frame wall they vibrate the drywall and 2×4s. Because there's nothing to absorb the sound, that vibration is transmitted through the stud wall and out the other side. One way to solve the problem is to add mass to the wall by screwing up another layer of drywall (½ in. should work fine). Even better is to add a layer of fiberboard—a particularly sound-deadening material—and then a second sheet of drywall. Instead of attaching it directly to the fiberboard, use metal furring strips, called resilient channels, to create an air gap between the second layer of drywall and the fiberboard. Then you can crank it up.

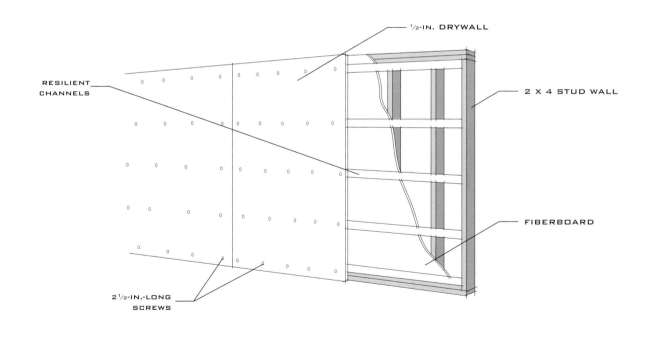

½-IN. DRYWALL

RESILIENT CHANNELS

2 X 4 STUD WALL

FIBERBOARD

2½-IN.-LONG SCREWS

To the Moon, Mars, and Beyond

"Honey, I'll be in the observatory," is the kind of thing you'll hear in the evenings around the Sharp household as Nelson heads to his home viewing tower to stare at the stars.

The observatory was built on a corner of the Sharp's Telluride, Colo., summer home like a private air traffic control tower poking up above the second-story roofline. From the front courtyard of the house, the observatory looks like a normal square room surrounded by windows rather than having the domed roof most people picture when they think observatory. That's the way Nelson

wanted it. Besides, he didn't have a choice. Local building codes prohibit domed roofs.

Inside the tower, the normalcy leaves off. Coming up through the floor is a large steel post supporting a round crow's nest that sits just under the hip roof. When Nelson wants to look at the night sky from a reclining chair in the crow's nest, he uses a software program to open a panel in the roof above his 16-in. Schmidt-Cassegrain Meade® telescope. He finds specific nebulae, comets, or exploding white giants by typing coordinates into his computer, which then swivels the platform, along with the entire roof, into place.

Nelson, who is a retired mechanical engineer and entrepreneur, has long had an interest in astronomy, though before creating his current setup the hobby was limited to squinting through small telescopes on tripods. When he sold his technical training business in 1999, he and

Who needs a domed roof to look at the stars? Not Nelson Sharp. A door lifts up in the hip roof of his observatory, then the whole thing swivels to position the telescope underneath.

Sharp built his Telluride, Colo., dream home and observatory in 2003 in the shadow of the San Juan Mountains.

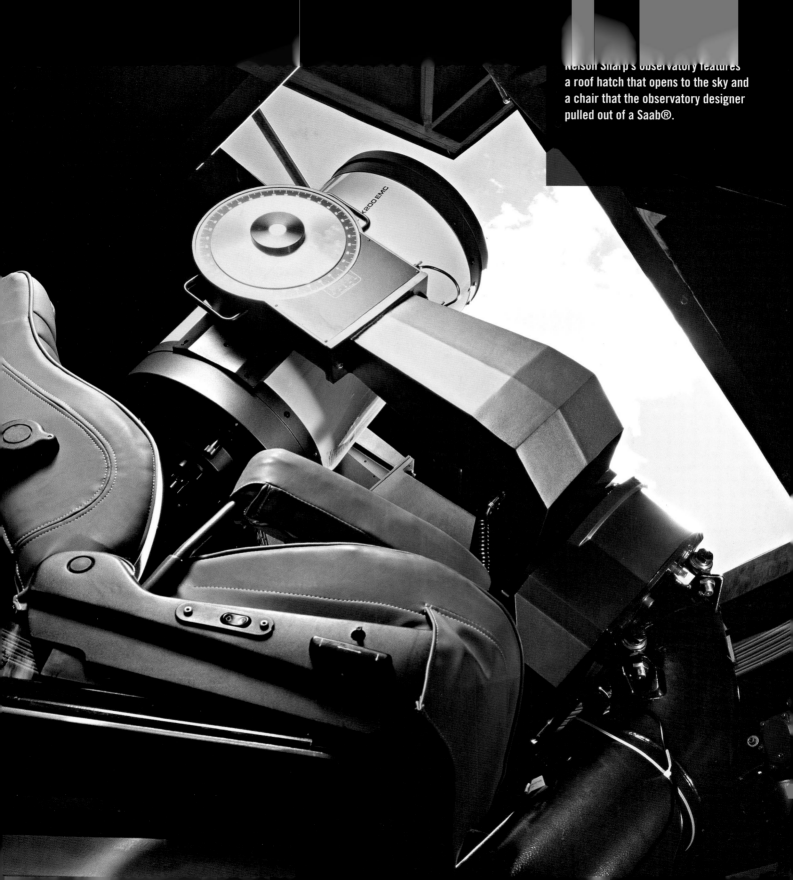

Nelson Sharp's observatory features
a roof hatch that opens to the sky and
a chair that the observatory designer
pulled out of a Saab®.

his wife decided to build the house in Colorado and add a real observatory. He hired architect Craig Melvin to design and build the house and tower. Patrick Meyer, a builder who constructed the University of Denver's Mt. Evan's Meyer-Womble Observatory, designed the hardware and the working parts of the viewing platform.

SPACE THE SWIVELS

Because the slightest vibration or bump can move the telescope light-years off target, Melvin and Meyer knew the crow's nest had to be perfectly rigid at all times. To accomplish that they attached the black metal post to its own concrete foundation pier, essentially making it a freestanding structure. The tower was built around it with an entirely separate foundation. Meyer then designed the swivel action of the crow's nest and the roof and wired the system so Nelson could control it through a remote computer (eventually Nelson wants to be able to use his office computer on the other side of the house).

Nelson not only looks at the stars; he photographs them too. Because the light is so far away and so faint, single exposures can sometimes take up to 20 minutes, which means on clear summer nights he might spend several hours searching through galaxies far from home. Talk about a heavenly manspace.

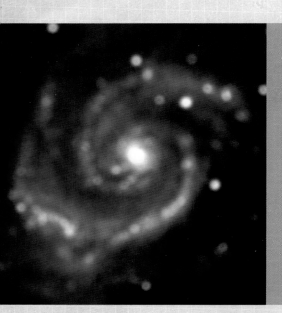

GEAR
SHOOTING STARS

When Nelson Sharp wants to locate and photograph a particular star or comet like the one he photographed here, he uses the North Star. The telescope is then calibrated to the star's position using computer software. By doing this, Sharp is able to establish an axis for his equipment so that it can compensate for the earth's rotation, an important consideration once you locate what you're looking for. It also allows him to find locations. Not surprisingly, many galaxies have been catalogued and assigned an "M," or Messier, number. Once he's calibrated, Sharp can enter the M number into his computer and the telescope will find it.

Sharp's 16-in. photographic Schmidt-Cassegrain Meade telescope is the largest, most sophisticated retail model available, with a price tag of around $20,000.

The observatory's crow's nest fits snugly in the ceiling without touching the wood around it. A computer program swivels the platform automatically to adjust for the earth's rotation.

Sharp controls the roof hatch and telescope positioning from this room in the observation tower. The mechanics for the mesh platform are housed inside the black steel post.

MR. MOON AND THE MOON

Matthew Moon spends so much time camping, skiing, and playing outdoors that it made sense for him to live outside too. His solution? Live in a teepee.

Granted, teepees are not normally known for their domestic conveniences. Moon, who is in his late 20s, has a full kitchen, plus a bathroom, a bed, and a giant woodstove. He can live as close to the land as possible and still shower, cook breakfast, and show up on time to his job as a high school music teacher in nearby Las Platas, N.M.

Living under a pile of canvas wasn't Moon's first plan of action. On a trip to Telluride two summers ago he caught a glimpse of a teepee owned by designer Ralph Lauren and decided to trade in his current abode—a mobile home—for a teepee. It would sit perfectly on his four-acre parcel, a bluff that overlooks sweeping wilderness.

When he got back home he sold the mobile home and ordered a teepee from Earthworks, a Colorado-based company. Before it arrived he prepared a level pad and built a secure shed to house his hot-water heater (his water comes from a well and he is hooked up to Las Platas's electrical grid). When the teepee's canvas and poles arrived, Moon and four friends erected it in six hours.

Living in the teepee has taken some getting used to. A little rain comes in through the top where the poles meet, but it falls only on the middle of the floor, which is covered in concrete pavers. Also, it gets cold in the winter, so Moon keeps the woodstove stoked from December to March. Still, he enjoys being so close to the weather and the land. He always has.

On Matthew Moon's teepee, 75 lb. of canvas wraps around 15 poles. The smoke flaps over the front door are laced together with traditional Native American cedar sticks.

A separate sheet of canvas called an *ozan* covers Moon's bed and bathroom to protect against rain that might leak in during heavy storms and to provide a small amount of insulation.

After Moon hikes or bikes in the sweeping New Mexican landscape, the teepee's quaint front door welcomes him home.

A 4-ft.-high canvas liner, seen behind Moon's kitchen, is strung up around the interior to keep wind and dust from blowing under the exterior canvas.

RAISING A MAN BARN

Like a phoenix rising from the flames, Chub Whitten's manspace was born from fire. After an old woodstove ignited the walls of his 1720 colonial in Ipswich, Mass., the commercial real estate agent rebuilt the house in 1999 with most of the insurance money he received. Instead of buying new furniture with the rest of it, he built a timber-frame barn where a little-used tennis court had stood.

Whitten had long wanted room enough on his property to house a woodshop. After the fire, Whitten hired Michael Doiron to rebuild the house and manage the construction of his new manspace. His brother Rob Whitten, an architect, came up with the design. Chub wanted a traditional-looking building to match his colonial-style house, and he wanted to build it with old-fashioned techniques. While demolishing a 19th-century warehouse he'd bought as a real estate investment, he discovered some 150-year-old 8-in. by 8-in. Douglas fir beams. After pouring a concrete

Whitten's barn is separated into three bays and two upstairs lofts. The middle bay opens at both ends with 12-ft.-high doors so he can drive his boat in through the front or back.

Chub Whitten adjusts a water ski out front of his 1,000-sq.-ft. timber-frame barn. The doors were modeled after those found on warehouses and slide open automatically.

slab, Doiron and Chub used the wood to construct a structure using mortise-and-tenon joints held together with wooden pegs. They sheathed the building with locally milled pine and fastened the boards with old-style steel-cut nails.

Whitten uses the space as a woodshop and to store cars and equipment, like his boat and skis. In the winter, he'll spend entire weekend days inside tinkering with his tools. He and his wife Nicole have a one-and-a-half-year-old daughter named Natalie, so Whitten's recent building projects have included a crib and a changing table. It gets cold inside the heaterless building during January and February, but Whitten just puts on another sweater. A woodstove is out of the question.

During the summer months, water skiing is Whitten's favorite thing to do, which means the barn isn't used for much more than storage from June to August.

Whitten's woodshop occupies one side of the barn. The floor is made out of 2¾-in. heart-pine boards he recovered from a demolition project.

PRESIDENTIAL MANSPACE

Poker and cigars go together as easily as beer and Monday Night Football. Poker and presidential politics, on the other hand, isn't such an easy match. For Harry Truman, the nation's 33rd president, playing cards was one of his favorite ways to wind down from the stress of the job. He just didn't like to talk about it during his two terms in the White House for fear that the public might not approve of a gambling commander-in-chief.

Truman's favorite spot to play cards was on the presidential yacht, the *Williamsburg* (see the photo below), which would steam up and down the Potomac in Washington, D.C., for entire weekends with Truman and his poker friends on board. Rumor has it the president liked to bluff and was prone to losing money more than winning it. Another favorite place to ante up was at the Little White House in Key West, Fla., where Truman spent 175 days during his presidency relaxing and doing the nation's business. In fact, the building still displays the leader's manspace—a round, wooden poker table with a green felt inner circle and chip holders cut into the sides. The table also had a custom cover that transformed the gambling site into a regular dining room flat top. For Truman and his wife Bess, certain things were best left hidden.

Once Upon a Shed

David Ballinger stumbled on the idea of a manspace at work. He'd been producing a home-improvement television show in England called *Changing Rooms* (the basis for the American show *Trading Spaces*), and on one of the episodes the cast was charged with making a backyard office shed. Unfortunately, the construction took too long, the finished product didn't look great, and it cost too much money. The episode was a disaster. "After the show I kept thinking, 'There's got to be a better way of doing this,'" says Ballinger. So he went home and started tinkering in his own backyard, some 40 miles northwest of Lon-

don. Before long he had come up with the Metroshed®, a 120-sq.-ft. glass-front rectangle with a flat roof made of a sturdy, clear acrylic called Lexan®.

Soon people in his neighborhood started inquiring about the shed. Some would stop him as he left for work. Others would leave their business cards on his car. Eventually he agreed to replicate the outbuilding for others. In a year he sold 26 of them. That's a healthy amount, even in Britain, where there's a long-established shed culture.

Ballinger has since moved to Florida, where he builds Metrosheds full time for clients around the country for about $7,000 each. The sheds are shipped as kits. When a kit arrives at a client's house, Ballinger flies a team of workers to the location to assemble the parts in a matter of hours (this is included in the price). He also built a Metroshed on his five-acre Orlando property for himself. When business is particularly hectic, he can go there to make a quiet phone call. It's also a place where he and his friends play poker or hang out. It may have taken Ballinger some work to create the Metroshed, but now the work stays outside.

Playing cards inside Ballinger's prefab poker room is like gambling in a small private clubhouse.

No manspace is complete without
a place to nap, even if it's just a
cozy chair in the corner.

Dave Ballinger's 8-ft. by 10-ft.
shed gets electrical power via a
large extension cord that plugs
into a 120-volt outlet—the same
needed for any large appliance.

FIVE

SPORTING

"A hot dog at the ballpark is better than a steak at the Ritz." — *Humphrey Bogart*

If you started talking to someone about a manspace, man room, or any other kind of man zone, chances are they would immediately think of a bunch of guys sitting around watching a big-screen TV, drinking beer, eating chips, and doing lots of yelling. Stereotypes can be so unfair. Anyone who thinks that's all guys do in their own rooms doesn't know what they're talking about. After all, guys don't just watch anything on TV while they drink, yell, scratch, and snack. They watch sports.

That said, watching sports isn't the only thing going on in sporting-themed manspaces. Take Corey Pandolph, a New York Yankees fan who transformed his dining room into a sports bar. Sure there's a TV, and no, he doesn't miss a game, but he also writes a syndicated comic strip about a woman from Brooklyn who moves to a small town in the Adirondack Mountains. When the game's not on, he'll pour himself a pint and sit down in his space to draw.

GETTING IN THE GAME

There are also the guys who bypass the TV altogether, preferring to play sports rather than watch them. Professional boxer Wayne McCullough got so tired of waiting for a turn at the gym that he built a boxing ring inside his garage. Businessman Mike Gilliland took a look at the fireplace chimney going up inside his home office and realized he could climb it. Then there's Austin, Tex., resident Donnie Knutson. With tattoos covering both arms and one creeping up the side of his neck, the former rockabilly band manager is certainly not your typical sports guy. Nonetheless, he installed a ten-pin bowling alley in his backyard and you can rest assured that it's not there just because it looks good.

Come to think of it, this chapter contains everything but a typical sports room with a big-screen TV, overstuffed couch, and team colors painted on the walls. There may be a standard ice-fishing cabin sitting over a hole in the ice, but add in the fact that it's part of a weekend festival in Minnesota that actually gives out a prize to the guy with the hairiest back and things get a little weird. The outdoor sportsmen in these pages aren't satisfied with the typical hunting cabin or trophy room—unless you consider it a normal thing to sleep in an open-air lean-to during a Colorado winter. That guy doesn't even have electricity for a TV in his manspace.

FLY PAD

Some men like to fish. Barry Beck can't *not* fish. What started at the age of nine tying fly lures in his parents' fishing goods shop has now become a full-blown obsession with fly fishing. Most of the year Beck and his wife, and fellow angler, Cathy teach and talk about fly fishing while guiding tours to New Zealand, Argentina, Alaska, and the American West. At times Beck will trade in his rod for a camera or a computer, but even then he's photographing and writing about angling. Not a day goes by that he isn't catching or trying to catch a fish.

On the rare occasions that he's at home in northeastern Pennsylvania, Beck can step out onto his front porch and cast his line into the trout-filled waters of Raven Creek. The house is hours away from the nearest airport, but he'd never trade the quiet life in the country for convenience. In fact, the great outdoors, more than the fish,

This imitation sculpin minnow, held in the tip of a vise, is used for underwater freshwater fishing. Big trout love these lures.

Barry Beck has been tying flies in his basement for 25 years to catch fish all over the world with his wife Cathy, one of the leading female anglers in the field.

Colorful spools of thread are in easy reach at this freshwater tying station. The meticulous work of fly tying requires a good light and a steady hand.

is what's held Beck's interest year after year and catch after catch for over three decades. Landing a 10-lb. trout is fun, he says, but hunting for it in the lush mountains of New Zealand is inspiring.

As he did as a boy, Beck still ties all his own flies. His basement in Pennsylvania is the workshop where he builds lures to give his travel clients and sell through the couple's website, www.barryandcathybeck.com. There's a saltwater tying station where he threads imitation shrimp and bait for bone fish and tarpon. Two other stations are set up to tie mayflies for trout, peacock bass, and other freshwater fish.

After being in the fishing business for 35 years, Beck has made plenty of friends who share his zeal for casting a line. When he and Cathy are gone, friends let themselves into the Pennsylvania house, tie flies in the basement, and fish. On busy weekends it's common to have anglers sleeping all over the house, including the basement, even if the Becks are a continent away.

Not surprisingly, Beck has plenty of good fish tales, but the best one includes a fish he didn't catch. He was hosting a group of fishermen on the Big Horn River in Montana. Among the group was a young minister who had been battling diabetes all his life to the extent that he was now going blind. The minister was a passionate fisherman, but because of his failing eyesight this fishing trip would be his last. During the expedition the minister landed the largest trout he'd ever caught and was so moved that he began to cry. "It was the happiest I've ever been to see someone catch a fish," says Beck. It's times like these that keep Beck's rod and reel close by and his eyes peeled for that next fishing adventure.

Triangular-shaped pieces of wire called thread bobbins hold spools of thread and make them easy to manage.

The lone saltwater tying station in Beck's basement stocks nail polish for paint and a beefy vise to hold bigger hooks.

The Swedish Sport of Sweating

Photographer Matthew Benson likes to sweat. As a boy he lived in Sweden's wintry port capital, Stockholm, where basking in saunas is a national health ritual. It helps improve blood circulation, and by sweating a person can cleanse the body of impurities. For Benson, taking a sauna is also a way to relax after hunching over negatives or squinting into a camera lens all day.

Getting a sauna of his own has taken some time and work. After he and his wife Heidi moved to a three-acre farm in New York's Hudson River Valley ten years ago, Benson was ready to build a small sweat room. First, though, he needed to fix up the main 19th-century farmhouse. Then he began personally renovating a collection of outbuildings, including a horse barn that he transformed into his photography studio. It wasn't until the couple decided to build a lap pool eight years later that Benson recognized his opportunity. He'd put a small dry sauna in the pool house.

Benson used salvaged wood for the 4-ft. by 8-ft. sweat room. Ironically enough, the 1-in. by 10-in. wood on the walls of the sauna came from an old icehouse, where 150 years ago the farm residents stored blocks of ice cut from the Hudson River. The inside of the door is made from worn and scratched boards he removed from the stalls inside the old horse barn.

The door to the sauna is located just off the pool house's sitting porch. Next to the door, behind the red-and-white-striped gate, is an outdoor shower that comes in handy after a dip in the pool.

Accoutrements inside the sauna include a wooden bucket and ladle to pour water on electrically heated volcanic rocks and produce rejuvenating steam. The back scrubber hangs from an antler.

A 12-ft. by 45-ft. pool is mere steps from the sauna. Benson's wife Heidi likes to swim laps while he sweats out the day's stress.

DRY HEAT

Because the sauna is a dry one (as opposed to a steam sauna) Benson uses an electric heater that warms a collection of stones and raises the temperature as high as 180°. There's room inside for three people, but Benson prefers to sweat alone after a long day in the office. Like the Swedes, he'll stay in the sauna for about 15 minutes before ladling some water onto the hot rocks inside the heater to produce steam. When he can't stand the heat any longer he takes a bracing jump in the cold pool just outside the door. "At that point there's a lot of screaming and yelping," says Benson. He repeats the process two or three times before rinsing off under the outdoor shower on the side of the pool house. When he's done, he puts on a terry-cloth robe and lays down on the chaise longue just outside the sauna door, rejuvenated and cleansed and ready for the next photography assignment or building project. Sweating keeps him going.

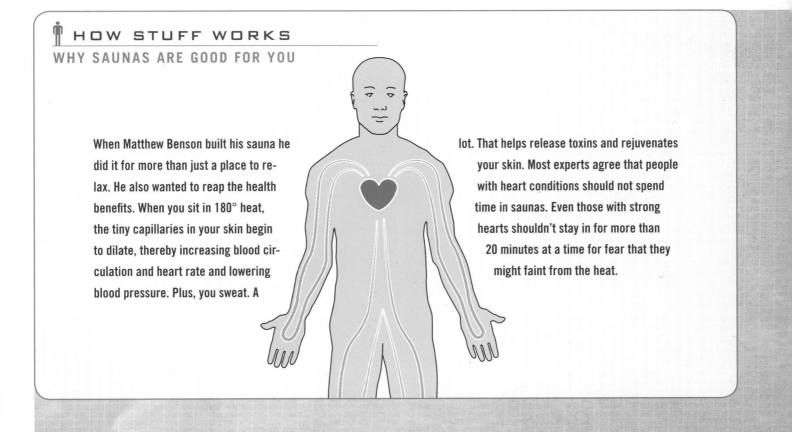

HOW STUFF WORKS
WHY SAUNAS ARE GOOD FOR YOU

When Matthew Benson built his sauna he did it for more than just a place to relax. He also wanted to reap the health benefits. When you sit in 180° heat, the tiny capillaries in your skin begin to dilate, thereby increasing blood circulation and heart rate and lowering blood pressure. Plus, you sweat. A lot. That helps release toxins and rejuvenates your skin. Most experts agree that people with heart conditions should not spend time in saunas. Even those with strong hearts shouldn't stay in for more than 20 minutes at a time for fear that they might faint from the heat.

TOTAL MAN SPACE

Before Curtis Berlind bought the *Go Getter*, a 75-ft. wooden tug-boat, it was languishing in its slip on the Oakland side of San Francisco Bay. The owner no longer had the time to use the boat, which was built in 1923, and couldn't afford its upkeep. Parts of the hull were deteriorating and vandals had broken in several times.

Berlind had been looking to trade his house near Berkeley for a boat. As a former naval officer, he had plenty of experience living at sea. He also knew the *Go Getter* was a good deal when he saw it. She was made entirely of Douglas fir and had a double hull. The interior had been refinished with loving perfection by the former owner before falling into disrepair. With the pilot house, the three rooms on deck, and the three rooms below, Berlind, who is single, had almost 1,000 sq. ft. to live and work in.

Dry-docking the boat in Sausalito, he had the hull inspected, repaired, and painted. But as anyone who knows boats can tell you, the work didn't stop there. With the ship in constant contact with saltwater, checking for peeling paint and the possibility of deteriorating wood is a constant job. After eight years living aboard the boat, Berlind is content to stay. In his office below deck he works as a corporate negotiator, helping companies settle out-of-court lawsuits. Being so close to the water also offers him easy access to his favorite sport—sea kayaking. For Berlind, paddling around the bay is like going for a walk around the block.

With his wooden tugboat, the *Go Getter*, in its slip at the end of a pier, Curtis Berlind has unimpeded views of San Francisco Bay and the Bay Bridge. He pays $800 a month for the spot.

The walls, floor, and trimwork inside the tugboat's head and main deck are made of Douglas fir. Resting against the wall are Berlind's naval officer's uniform and his mandolin.

In the ship's galley or kitchen—one of the three rooms inside the main deck in addition to a bunk room and a living room—Berlind keeps a propane-fueled 1920s-era Wedgewood stove.

A MANSPACE FOR THE BOYS

Some men have enough room for themselves and they don't need a manspace. Instead, they simply build one for their kids. Such is the case with this investment banker in Massachusetts who bought a 15-acre property with a house, a log cabin, a guest house, and an old barn. All the structures needed work, and the barn was in such bad shape it had to be demolished and rebuilt. Instead of including the hay lofts in the new design, the banker's architect Chip Dewing outfitted the new barn with half a basketball court, an exercise room, a pool table, and an apartment. In short, he created a man barn.

Though the banker shoots hoops on occasion, his three sons and their friends are the ones who have gotten the most use out of the court over the years. All three were day students at a nearby boarding school. The other boarders would often stay for weekends, turning the barn into a home away from home. When not shooting baskets on the ground floor, the boys could hang out on the second floor and play pool or head up to the third floor to lift weights and watch a game on TV.

All that said, the barn isn't always overrun with kids or sports. The banker goes there to read a book by one of the fireplaces or work out. He and his wife also use the basketball court to host large fundraisers and other charity functions (together they are on the boards of at least six different organizations). Each year they host a Christmas party for the neighborhood with more than 300 people. A man's space is indeed his own, but no one ever said he couldn't share it.

The exposed fir timbers of the barn's structure frame a sitting area just off the basketball court where the owner likes to relax and read after a workout.

Though the old barn was demolished, the architect raised a new one on the original footprint to match the colonial style of the 300-year-old main house.

Architect Chip Dewing salvaged the floor of this Massachusetts basketball court from a gym in Maine. Upstairs is a bar and exercise room. Downstairs leads to a swimming pool.

FISHING AND DRINKING: THE HOLE STORY

Sitting around a hole inside a plywood cabin on a frozen lake is the type of cruel fun men like to have. There's beer, good jokes, stories, more beer, and even some fishing that goes on. The fishing part, though, is often just an excuse for the rest of it.

Nowhere is this phenomenon on greater display than at Lake Leech in Walker, Minn., home of the annual Eelpout Festival. The weekend hoopla in February draws about 1,200 guys from the region each year. Unofficially (and, some say, the real reason for the get-together), guys come to hang out and generally make magnificent fools of themselves. Officially, they come to see which team and individual can catch the most and the biggest eelpout, a barely edible bottom feeder in the dogfish family. Events include a "polar plunge," where folks go for a below-freezing February dip (the governor of Minnesota participated last year). Prizes are also given for "the most lavish eelpout bivouac." In other words, whoever has the best manspace wins.

Setups range from the basic (a homemade shed with a moose head tacked to the front) to the lavish (a log cabin on sleds with a generator and a TV to watch sports). One year, a group of local limnologists (scientists who study inland bodies of water) from Bemidji State University turned their camp trailer into the "Pout-ological Research Center," complete with a poster presentation showing the number of pout caught per beer consumed. They declined to eat their haul, opting instead for a deep-fried turkey.

Gilliland's office is a short stroll from his house and serves as the home base for both his concrete climbing wall and Sun Flower Market, a natural-foods chain that he runs.

WHERE THERE'S A WALL, THERE'S A WAY

In his younger years, before becoming a successful businessman, Mike Gilliland loved rock climbing. Later, when his natural-foods supermarket Wild Oats took off and became a popular chain, his climbing really fell off, so to speak (he has since sold Wild Oats and started another natural-foods chain, Sun Flower Market). So when he was watching construction workers in his new office build a fireplace with a three-story indoor chimney, his spider senses began to reawaken and he thought, "I could climb that wall."

Because of his earlier interest in climbing, Gilliland knew of Monolithic Sculpture, Inc., a Boulder, Colo., group of engineers, sculptors, and rock jocks who build walls around the country for climbing gyms and festivals. Monolithic also does high-end private walls, but costs can be high so their clients are limited to those who have the space and can afford it. Gilliland fit the bill on both fronts.

WALL OF PAIN

Monolithic's Ty Foose designed and helped build Gilliland's concrete wall. It starts above the fireplace mantel and extends past the second-floor balcony and into a cupola above the roof rafters. The company reinforced the wood frame around the standard fireplace chimney and used it as a base. They then bolted on structural foam and sprayed it with three layers of concrete in the same

The Boulder, Colo., headquarters for Gilliland's natural-foods business and personal climbing wall hosts several employees during the day and occasional parties at night.

The finger and toe holds are manufactured by the company that built the wall and can be moved to create easy or more challenging climbs.

way workers might spray concrete to create a swimming pool. A team of artists then came in to mold and chisel the concrete to include natural-looking seams that mimic crack formations. Climbers can jam their fingers and toes into the seams in order to make their way up the wall.

As a final touch, Foose and his workers painted the wall to look like granite and attached toe and finger holds.

Now that Gilliland has his wall, he can climb any time. He does, however, have to contend with his kids and his kids' friends. In fact, during the days Gilliland's wife uses the office as a classroom to home-school a group of children from the neighborhood. The wall is sometimes used during recess. Ropes are left in place and climbing shoes are nearby in case anyone working in the office has the urge to flex their spider skills.

 GEAR
ROCK ON

Even though Mike Gilliland's wall was made to look just like nothing more than a rock, Monolithic Sculpture, Inc.'s Ty Foose used a combination of computer modeling and artisan craft to make sure of it. First Foose sketched out some concepts on paper. Then he and a team made a 3-D model, which was scanned into a computer and upsized to a full-scale blueprint. Sculptors used that to carve the basic shape of the wall out of structural foam. After three layers of concrete were sprayed onto the foam, the sculptors shaped it by hand (they had about six hours before it set up). Last, painters applied six coats of paint and stain to make the rock look like weathered granite.

Gilliland doesn't even have to move the furniture out of the way to scale the fireplace, but no one has yet tried to climb the chimney with a fire blazing.

If the front of the wall is occupied, climbers can do a short route on the back side, starting from the second-floor balcony.

THE BOXER

When you're an Olympic silver medalist and a former Bantamweight WBC World Champion, you shouldn't have to wait in line at the gym. But that's just what boxer Wayne "Pocket Rocket" McCullough had to do for years just to get in the ring in Las Vegas, where he lives and works. "It was like you had to take a ticket even if you were training for a big fight," he says. In 1999 he transformed his garage into a gym and never looked back.

McCullough, who learned his trade as a boy on the tough streets of Belfast in Northern Ireland, turned pro after winning the silver medal at the Barcelona Olympics in 1992. In 1995, with his wife Cheryl as his manager, he won the WBC Bantamweight championship belt in Japan. After several more years of training and fighting (in which he was the runner-up for the championship in two different weight classes), McCullough couldn't wait around at the local gyms anymore.

The boxer found a company in California to come construct a standard-size ring in his three-car garage. At 20 ft. by 20 ft., it fits perfectly across two car bays. In the third bay, McCullough had a steel beam installed as a ceiling joist to hold a heavy punching bag. He added a speed bag next to that. Then, to replicate the atmosphere of the old boxing gyms of Belfast, he covered the walls with fight posters of famous contests, including some of his own, and photographs of him posing with other well-known boxers.

Everyone in McCullough's Las Vegas neighborhood has a garage, but his is the only one with a boxing ring in it.

The only vehicle able to fit in Wayne McCullough's three-car garage turned boxing ring is his Harley. The rest of the space is used as a training center for his next professional fight.

As a side job, McCullough is a personal trainer and uses his garage to help individuals get in shape and feel the thrill of being in the ring.

McCullough has also claimed the "Rocket Room," just off of the garage. It's where he watches fights with his buddies and shows off his medals, trophies, and championship belts.

McCullough wanted the garage to feel like an old Irish gym, so he put up fight posters. His attempts to make it dirty and smelly have been unpopular with wife Cheryl.

Next to the water cooler, McCullough framed and hung his collection of photographs of him posing with boxing champs like Joe Frazier and George Foreman.

HOME SCHOOLING

Now there's no more waiting in line. Cheryl, who works in a small office above the garage, might go downstairs and tell McCullough to turn the music down (he likes it full blast when he's training). Sometimes his eight-year-old daughter Wynona will jump in the ring to play. One time when McCullough was wrapping up a session Wynona spontaneously grabbed some gloves and started punching the heavy bag. "I'll feel sorry for her first boyfriend," the boxer says with a chuckle. Mostly though, the family knows when a tough fight is coming up and they let McCullough have his space.

As a side job, he does some personal fitness training, so he uses the ring with his clients. Occasionally the champ lets other fighters come train in his gym, and before big fights he likes to invite a journalist or two along with a few friends to come watch him spar. Otherwise, not even the cars are allowed in McCullough's garage when he's boxing.

VICTORY LAP
CHAMPIONSHIP POINTS

Wayne "Pocket Rocket" McCullough's professional record is 27–6 with 18 knockouts. He has fought for the WBC Championship in three weight classes, Bantamweight (115 lb. to 118 lb.), Super Bantam (118 lb. to 122 lb.), and Featherweight (122 lb. to 126 lb.), winning the Bantamweight title in 1995. After that fight he defended his title twice before sacrificing it to move up in weight class. Since then he has been the runner-up in six title fights, each time taking the current champ the distance. McCullough's toughness and persistence in the face of defeat has earned him a loyal following and a billing in the British press as the best Irish export since Guinness® beer.

Old signs and sports memorabilia line the walls inside Corey Pandolph's diminutive dining room bar. The décor was inspired by his and his wife's favorite watering hole, Gritty McDuff's in Portland, Maine.

DRINKING IN
THE BOYS' ROOM

For cartoonist and baseball enthusiast Corey Pandolph, building a sports bar inside his Portland, Maine, house wasn't as difficult as other married men imagine it must have been. For one, he didn't have to convince his wife, Kristen, who is a lifelong Oakland A's fan. Every year the two travel to a different baseball park in the country with the goal of eventually visiting them all. Corey has seen 12 so far; Kristen, 14. The problem is when Kristen wants to watch the A's play on TV at the same time as Corey's New York Yankees. That's when it's up to Corey to find someplace else to go. Usually he heads for the dining room.

The tiny 9-ft. by 10-ft. space is in the corner of the Pandolphs' 1,100-sq.-ft. house and has doorways into the kitchen and living room. Used to be that it was a bit of an eyesore. That was before Corey ripped up the carpet, put down a tongue-and-groove pine floor, and painted

Photos of Pandolph's grandfather, Chuck Pandolph, an Olympic bobsledder, hang in the bar. Chuck won a silver medal at the Lake Placid World Championships in 1961, as advertised in Corey's vintage poster.

1961 WORLD BOBSLED CHAMPIONSHIPS

FEB. 11-12
FEB. 18-19

LAKE PLACID, NEW YORK

the walls red. To finish the room, he cut prestained pine boards for the window trim. For the bar and liquor cabinet, he harvested some old barn wood from a friend's property. Martini-glass cutouts in the pine doors offer a clue to what's behind them. The working beer tap draws from a full-size keg in a refrigerator in the basement—a setup known to some as a "keg-o-rator." Corey ran a line through the floor and up into the cabinet, using a carbon-dioxide tank to carbonate and pressurize the flow.

Amazingly, the bar, a table with two chairs, and a television mounted high in one corner take up only half the room. Opposite that, a fold-up dining table hangs on the wall, ready to seat six for dinner, which is often of the liquid variety when Corey has his buddies over to watch the game.

The television may be small, but it does the trick when there's a can't-miss game on. Like any good barkeep, Pandolph keeps ketchup, mustard, and mayo on the table.

The baseballs above the bar were signed by players on the Seadogs, Portland's AA team, where Pandolph works as a groundskeeper.

Gone Fishin'

Cale Bradford grew up fishing with his father. When he got older he fished with friends, sometimes traveling to different continents in search of exotic waters. More than the catch, Bradford always preferred the camaraderie that came with fishing. Eventually, he and his friends got too busy with family and work to take the yearly fishing trip. Bradford, who is the vice president of a health insurance company near St. Louis, began to pine for a place of his own where he could cast his line and invite buddies over for a casual weekend fish. That's when he bought a small grain and timber farm in Perryville, Mo., through which runs Celine Creek, one of the state's premiere smallmouth bass fishing streams.

The decision to buy the property, which included a ranch-style house, was spurred by the fact that Bradford's wife, Rocío Romero, is an architect who builds prefabricated homes. She needed a place to build prototypes, one

Bradford bought land on both sides of Celine Creek to keep his fishing cabin as private as possible. Without a phone line or cell phone reception, the cabin is even more remote.

Bradford enjoys having his friends over to fish and hang out so much that he's adding electricity and plumbing to the building to turn it into a guest house.

Friends come from far and wide to attend Bradford's annual hog roast.

To leave no doubt that the space is his, Bradford put in an early 1960s Sears and Roebuck fireplace, a 1940s-era cigarette dispenser, and a propaganda poster depicting German airplanes bombing New York.

of which she calls the "Fish Camp," a utilitarian, 12-ft. by 24-ft. steel-sided rectangle with a shed roof, fixed Lexan clerestory windows, sliding front doors, and a big deck. Bradford knew just the spot where she could build it: casting distance from the creek. His only request was that once it was built, the place be his.

True to her word, Romero left the Fish Camp to Bradford once the building was finished. Because Celine Creek can expand unpredictably in heavy rains, the Fish Camp was set on a high bank and put on raised piers. With such sandy soil near the river the piers were made extra thick—2 ft. in diameter—and sunk 4 ft. into the ground. Initially, Bradford didn't bother running an

underground electricity line to the outpost or even adding plumbing for fear the water would wash everything away. He has since taken a chance and added both. He quickly outfitted the one-room structure with the midcentury furniture, accessories, and propaganda posters that he collects.

Bradford hardly misses an opportunity to have coffee and read the newspaper on the Fish Camp deck on weekend mornings. He's also fond of barbecuing for friends. Once a year he throws a hog roast, with 200 guests, kegs of beer, and plenty of pulled-pork sandwiches. He also manages to fish at the Fish Camp, but only when he has the time.

After Rocío Romero built the prototype for her husband Cale Bradford's fishing cabin, she began selling Fish Camp kits. The kit comes with wall, floor, and roof panels (they are all made of Structurally Insulated Panels or SIPs), windows, and doors. Romero also throws in a T-shirt, along with video instructions. All the panels are fastened with screws. Buyers have to supply their own foundation. The cost for a Fish Camp kit is under $20,000, and it takes just two people a few days to erect after the foundation is set.

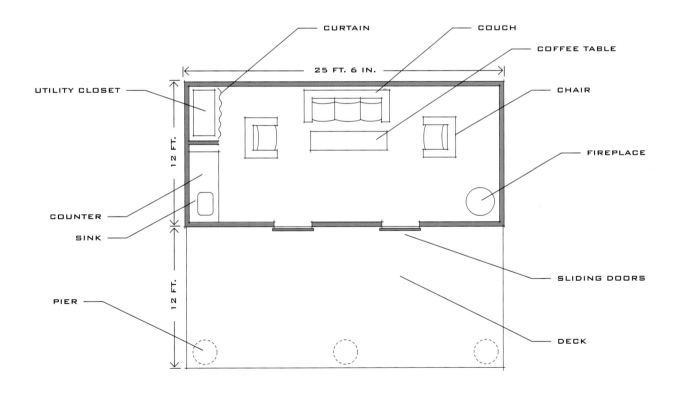

A BACKYARD BOWLING SPACE

A man can get a lot done with the right resources, and Austin resident Donnie Knutson is a resourceful man. For ten years he traveled the world as a road manager for rockabilly songwriters Dale Watson and Hank Williams III. When they needed a new amplifier in Western Australia, Knutson found it. If they were missing a microphone in Eastern Europe, he tracked one down.

When he and his future wife, Andee, bought a 1960 ranch-style house ten minutes north of downtown Austin, Tex., Knutson used the same get-things-done attitude to carve out a space of his own in his backyard. He began

Knutson says the halftime horn button is a favorite option for friends keeping score on the scoreboard's control box. Bocci balls replace full-sized bowlers in the nine-pin games.

Donnie Knutson was inspired to have an outdoor bowling alley after seeing English lawn bowling on a trip to Australia.

hanging Christmas lights and filling the area with folk art and found oddities. Where most people might have seen an old clothesline strung between two rusty old posts, Knutson saw a long stretch of unimpeded space—perfect for a bowling alley.

Growing up in a suburb of Detroit, he had spent a lot of time bowling. On most Friday nights he was at the local alley with his father, who belonged to a bowling league. In junior high, Knutson was on the bowling team. Andee was not impressed with his plan for a backyard alley, but he persisted. While tracking down some props for the media production company where he works, he found an old electric scoreboard from a high school gym with a working control box. He hauled it home in his baby-blue 1970 Ford pickup and the backyard bowling alley was born.

After digging up the clothesline posts, Knutson bought some Astroturf®, rolled it out, and cut it to size. He then glued it down to the concrete pavers that the previous owner had installed under the clothesline. To finish the space, he trimmed the lane with rock beds made out of landscaping timbers and limestone gravel. The scoreboard was hung on a garden shed at the end of the alley. In a single afternoon, the project was complete.

Now Knutson notices that when he and Andee throw parties most of the men gravitate to the bowling alley (an outdoor bar sits right next to it). And though Andee may not have taken up the sport, she has warmed to its presence at her house. "She's always the first person to tell people we have a bowling alley in the backyard," says Knutson. For him, bowling a few frames when no one's around is a great way to wind down and set his mind to the next backyard project.

Vintage bowling pins line Knutson's backyard alley. For actual games he uses nine 10-in. pins he found at Restoration Hardware. After replacing a few bulbs, the scoreboard was as good as new.

Knutson takes back roads and alleyways home from work in search of odd junk and found art. This lounge seat was made from the front seat of an old feed truck.

INTO THE WILD

On snowy winter nights Ken Pieper will take an extra blanket with him when he's sleeping in his Adirondack-style lean-to about 100 yd. behind his house in the Colorado Rockies. Usually he'll stay just one night, unless he and one of his sons have just gotten back from an elk hunt. Then he might stay two days, sleeping on the raised platform behind the log walls and roof that manage to keep the wind off, if not the cold. With elk steaks sizzling and hot coffee warming over the fire pit, coal oil lamps light the evening's conversations.

Pieper, who builds luxury homes, needed a place to escape to when the pressures of the business got to be too much. Having a rustic building was a way to get as close to nature as possible—his 6-acre property abuts miles and miles of undeveloped land that leads into a national forest. To take full advantage of the landscape, he decided to build the lean-to in the rough-hewn log and timber-frame Adirondack style. He and his wife are members of Adirondack Architectural Heritage and he wanted something in the style for his backyard retreat.

Several years ago he bought a model of a traditional lean-to on one of his Heritage Society trips with the idea of recreating it for himself. The following summer he hired a guy to do exactly this, using trees and rocks from his property for the frame and foundation. Once it was built, Pieper stocked the place with a feather mattress and some Adirondack antiques. On Sundays he'll often take a book up to the lean-to and read and nap in the afternoons. It's also a perfect place to enjoy a cigar and a snifter of cognac. Then, when hunting season starts, he'll bring the extra blankets. The snow can really stack up sometimes.

On warm summer days Pieper's wife will hang out with him in the lean-to as if they were camping far away, rather than a mere 100 yd. from their back door.

Ken Pieper's Colorado lean-to is out-fitted with antiques he bought on visits to New York's Adirondack Mountains. The structure is made entirely out of wood harvested from his property.

SIX

WORKING

"Money is better than poverty, if only for financial reasons." — *Woody Allen*

A workshop or home office is probably the oldest type of manspace in the history of men-only rooms. That may be because it doesn't take too much cajoling for a man to convince his wife that he needs to make some money. Even then, upgrading out of the garage isn't a certainty even if the rest of the family agrees not to drive the car in there until the end of the workday. Still, both animator Walt Disney and Apple Computer founder Steve Jobs started their operations out of the garage and they did all right.

In the past, however, working at home was what men usually did when they were between jobs or when they were young with nothing to lose. The reality was most guys in their garages would rather have been at the office earning a steady paycheck. Today, working for yourself at home still may not be the first choice for lots of men, but for those who can manage it, it's an appealing option. For one, the commute is short. Second, it's a great way to be available and unavailable at the same time. In other words, you can be home to greet the

kids when they come home from school, but you can also hang the "do not disturb" sign on the doorknob when you need to get down to business.

What's also different about working at home is the space itself. In Utah, architect Hank Louis works out of a grain silo that he converted into an office. In Seattle, filmmaker David Wild has created a minimalist cube called The Brain, which he uses to generate fresh ideas. These aren't exactly Mike Brady–style offices off the front hallway.

Perhaps the original work-at-home man and the manspace he works in are the artist and his studio. In this chapter you'll find sculptors, writers, and painters who have carved out creative niches—literally and figuratively. Charlie Ringer, a sculptor in Montana, commandeered a cheese factory for his first manspace. Thirty-five years later, he owns a compound of three buildings, including a state-of-the-art metalworking shop that he uses to cut, grind, and weld metal sculptures for customers around the country. It goes to show that if you give a man his space, he'll produce.

A PAINTER'S PLACE

Scott Anderson paints landscapes in the plein air style of French Impressionists like Claude Monet and Auguste Renoir. Like those masters, who set up their easels in fields and on country roads, capturing the light at a specific time of day is essential to his painting. Unfortunately for Anderson, light was not in abundant supply in the Minneapolis basement studio he shared with his wife Kristi, a graphic designer. For that matter, neither was ventilation. Because there were so few windows, the solvents from the oil paint he used became a health issue.

The Andersons talked with their good friend, architect Robert Gerloff, about replacing Scott and Kristi's falling-down garage, which is located in one of Minneapolis's historic neighborhoods, with a new one equipped with a painting studio for Scott. Strict neighborhood covenants proved to be the most challenging part of the job. By code, the shape and style of the garage roof had to mimic that of the Andersons' main house, which had a traditional gable roof with a steep pitch. Because they couldn't put a second story on the garage (also a code issue) they designed the studio to fit under the roof, but with such steep sides there wouldn't be much room to work. Gerloff's solution was to open up the space with large dormers on the north and south sides. This also provided Anderson with much-needed natural light.

Anderson's studio is so well lit that he uses it both as a place to paint and as a gallery to exhibit his work. In the evenings his painter friends come over to drink scotch and talk art. For her part, Kristi has the basement all to herself and she's happy to have the paint fumes gone. She has wondered, though, if the space over the garage wouldn't make a good yoga studio instead.

When Anderson wants to paint, the studio is only steps away from the main house. On summer evenings he and his friends gather on the small second-story deck.

The shed dormer on the north side is taller than the one on the south side of the garage so that Anderson can take advantage of the added exposure.

Behind Anderson's easel and palette—an old cutting board on top of an antique end table—the roofline angles sharply through the space. Architect Robert Gerloff built half-walls to provide storage nooks for his client's canvases.

A Bard in Bear Country

Before architect and writer Lawson Drinkard and his wife decided to move to Montana from Virginia last year, he needed a room to write in. The couple already had a small cabin and a piece of land near Billings where they'd vacationed for the previous 15 summers. The cabin barely accommodated the two of them and their teenage daughter, though, and Drinkard needed a quiet room in which to string sentences together.

The cabin was situated on a beautiful piece of property near the mountains and a glacial stream. One year during their vacation, friend Terry Baird called Drinkard up and asked him if he wanted an old homesteader's cabin he'd seen behind a local saddle shop. With the roof falling in, the place was prime for demolition. Drinkard eyed its hand-hewn logs, which dated at least as far back as the 1920s, admiring their heft and aesthetic quality. Drinkard bought the logs for $800. The next day he, Baird, and five other guys dismantled the cabin and hauled it back to Drinkard's property in three pickup trucks.

Over the winter Baird restacked the cabin and added a roof and a wraparound porch. He also cut fir planks for the floor inside, then ran electric and phone lines from the Drinkards' cabin. The next summer, Drinkard chinked the new cabin with an elastomeric mud compound that seals the gaps between the logs and keeps the Montana field mice out. He and his wife later moved to Montana full time. With their daughter in college, the cabin offers enough space, and with the writing room complete, Drinkard has an ideal home office with only the sounds of nature to contend with.

Now Drinkard works year-round in the cabin. During the winter months he uses a propane stove, which heats the place in five minutes. There is a futon couch that can accommodate guests, but not many accept Drinkard's offers of hospitality when they find out there's no bathroom in the place.

Drinkard enhanced the cabin's rusticity by keeping the interior wood unstained and the floor unsanded. Cleaning consists of sweeping dirt into cracks between the floor planks once a year.

Lawson Drinkard and his wife often use the cabin's porches to entertain guests or to sit and read or paint landscapes of the surrounding mountains. Inside it's all his.

A Studio
in the Stables

Photographer Matthew Benson never knew he was handy until he bought property outside of New York City. Ten years later, he's completely restored the 19th-century farm that he and his wife Heidi own in the Hudson River Valley. Benson worked on a barn, a greenhouse, an icehouse, and a two-stall horse stable that he's transformed into his photography studio. For that job he didn't just hang drywall or build partition walls like many weekend warriors. Benson carefully salvaged and reused the original materials, then added carpentry details worthy of a seasoned craftsman.

The 44-year-old photographer renovated the horse barn on weekends while he lived in the city during the week. His first order of business was to take apart the stalls. Then he carefully pried away the interior wallboards from the frame and numbered each one so he could later reinstall them in the same order. After opening up the walls, he wired the building with electricity and cable and added insulation. To accommodate his photography business, Benson added a loft on the south end of the barn to store equipment in and a peaked window on the north end to bring in valuable natural light.

DOWNING'S INFLUENCE
Inspired by 19th-century landscape architect and Gothic Revivalist Andrew Jackson Downing, Benson also wanted to add ornamentation and charm to the otherwise plain building. He removed the stall doors and replaced them with glass patio doors. Then he photocopied one of Downing's 19th-century fleur-de-lis gingerbread patterns, enlarged it, and traced it onto a 2-in. by 12-in. piece of spruce. Next, he cut out the pattern using a circular saw and router. He carved the finials on a lathe and glued them in place.

The eclectic furnishings in the horse-barn-turned-studio come from local auctions and include a red Empire couch and a Danish parlor stove that Benson put on a slab of bluestone.

Benson took the original stall doors, cut them in half, and used them as shutters on either side of the new patio doors to his studio.

Now that the Bensons and their two kids Daisy and Miles live in the country full time, Benson is either at work or at play. He enjoys being able to be at home with his kids, but also having a place to go to when he needs some peace and quiet. "The studio is enough of a separate space where it's someplace I can go and not be disturbed," he says. Taking up carpentry has been a great career move.

Benson built in a bank of book-shelves over his farm-table computer desk. The top shelves were peaked to reflect the Gothic Revival theme Benson adopted for the entire renovation.

The railings on the loft were part of the original horse stalls. In addition to restoring old buildings, Benson also makes furniture, including the green armoire with glass doors and a flat file.

The gingerbread adornment Matthew Benson added to the gable ends of his studio was inspired by landscape architect Andrew Jackson Downing, who lived in the Hudson River Valley in the 1830s, not far from where Benson lives now. Downing championed the American Gothic Revival style, which became known in some parts of the country as "Carpenter's Gothic" because of its highly ornamental and intricately crafted wood elements. The trimwork has roots in the early 1800s in England, where people dolled up Georgian buildings with the romantic detail, but was at the height of popularity in the late 19th and early 20th centuries on English and American Victorian homes.

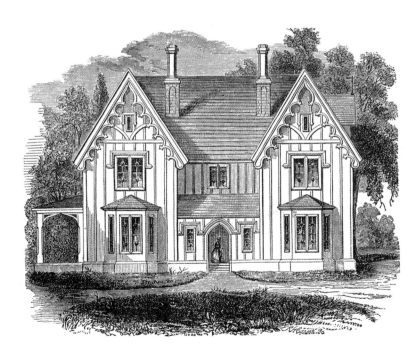

Northern light coming through a bank of raised windows illuminates a collection of DeWitt's clay and bronze sculptures.

A Sculpted Space

When 70-year-old artist Floyd Tennison DeWitt moved back to his native Montana 15 years ago after studying and making sculpture in Holland, he was a little miffed about studio options. Apparently, in Montana realtors hear "garage" when you ask for studio space. For years he made do working in these garages, but they were always too cramped and dim, and inevitably they ended up doubling as storage.

Eventually the frustration got to be too much and DeWitt decided to buy. His new home, a place in Bozeman, was surrounded by two acres. There was nowhere for him to work at first but there was plenty of room to expand. So he did. The result was a 4,000-sq.-ft. rectangle located off the west side of his house that captures plenty of northern light. To combat the cold Montana winters, he poured a concrete floor with radiant heating.

ART ALL AROUND

Now he says his main concern is finding a place to keep materials so they don't junk up the shop. At any given time he can be working on as many as 30 pieces and needs plenty of room to spread out. His creations range in size from items as small as a coffee cup to those about 5 ft. high. DeWitt's bronze sculptures begin life as clay and wax models that he forms using his hands or whatever happens to be lying around—sticks, pliers, or a carpenter's rasp. His subject matter varies widely, though a theme common to much of his work is passion and strength. Horses, homesteaders, and symphony conductors are a small sampling of the figures that have captured his eye. DeWitt says he's been working on one sculpture for 40 years and still isn't satisfied. At least now he doesn't have to worry about finding a space to perfect it.

The artist always works in front of a mirror to give the sculpture a sense of distance and objectivity. The figure he's working on is modeled after the conductor of the local symphony.

You're Not the Boss of Me

Perhaps the only thing better than making money doing what you love is being your own boss. David Kimura gets to do all three in his Seattle manspace.

Long an avid rock climber and hiker, the entrepreneur decided one day that he couldn't find gear that performed just the way he wanted it to. A zipper would break on a pack, for example, or he'd run out of fuel too soon for his camping stove. So he decided to make his own. Sure, these days he spends half his time sitting in front of a computer or a sewing machine, but the other half is spent in the back country testing the prototypes. Should he feel the need to spend an extra day "testing" the gear, the only person he has to clear it with is himself.

Kimura's office is steps from his house and, conveniently, right on the edge of a wilderness park with plenty of hiking trails. Originally the place was just a roof held

With his house on a hill in the background, Kimura can pursue his outdoor gear inventions a short hike away in his open-air studio.

The dark wood beams in David Kimura's backyard workshop were salvaged from an old chocolate factory and installed by the previous owner. Kimura added electricity and finished out the interior himself.

up by four posts. The previous owner had intended to turn it into a glassblowing shop but didn't finish it. Kimura closed in the walls, added some windows and an extra-wide doorway, and installed a laminate wood floor with radiant heat. Planning to use it as a full-time workshop, he insulated the walls and roof. Because he has a limited amount of room he installed castors on the legs of his worktable and shelving system so they can be moved easily.

Currently, Kimura has no employees, but he doesn't really need them. His job is to design a prototype using 3-D computer software, drawings, and cloth patterns.

Once he gets the specifics down, he'll build the prototype with a sewing machine and have a local shop fabricate any metal shapes he might need. After some testing to work out the kinks, he'll find a buyer and then have the piece of equipment manufactured.

One item he thinks will take off is a compact camping stove that burns only twigs, pine cones, and leaves so that its owner never has to worry about packing in or running out of fuel. Kimura has a patent pending on the invention and can personally vouch for the stove's efficiency. He's used it plenty of times already and plans to use it plenty more. He can do that. He's the boss.

GEAR
NO FUEL-ING AROUND

Kimura's camping stove, which is as yet unnamed, could be the best thing for overnight campers since the invention of the blow-up mattress. Instead of packing in kerosene, propane, or some other bulky fuel stove, campers can simply use the twigs and pine cones near their tent site. The stove works like a chimney, which draws fire and heats up. The holes in the side of the metal tube draw air in and naturally stoke the fire. They also let campers feed pencil-size sticks into the fire. Kimura hopes to start with two models—one small and a larger one that folds down.

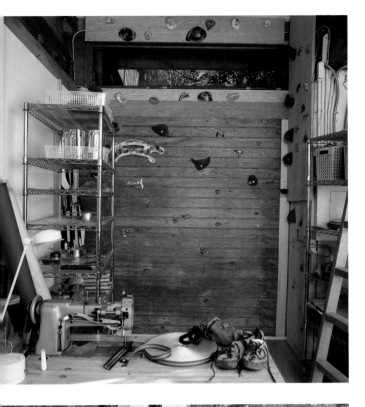

An avid climber, Kimura can practice his moves right in his studio when the indoor rock gyms get crowded in the winter.

Sewing machines in a man-space? Only if they're the industrial kind and used for stitching backpacks. Colorful thread spools and seam tape around the machines are used to decorate and reinforce the gear.

Kimura's worktable is stocked with nylon pack cloth below and riveters and sheet-metal cutters and punchers—all needed to make things like this small stove and pack panel.

OFFICE IN THE ROUND

In the canyons around Park City, Utah, architect and pro-
fessor Hank Louis does a lot of experimenting. His graduate studio class at the University of Utah has designed
and built a band shell and a park for the city as well as
sustainable low-income housing for the local Navajo reservation. That's why when it came time to build a backyard
home office for his private firm, Gigaplex, he erected a
grain silo. He needed a place to work but he also wanted
to test out the idea that a silo could be an affordable
place to live. The structure turned out to be a fine
housing option, though after finishing out the interior,
not a cheap one.

He bought the 24-ft.-dia. silo from an industrial farm
catalogue for $5,500. Because it came unassembled,
Louis put it together in sections, which required some
unorthodox construction techniques. First, Louis and a
crew poured a round concrete slab embedded with radiant

The windows and doors fit into an
interior-insulated frame of 2×6s.
Copper has been molded over the
exterior trim, and the entire two-
story building is heated by a radiant
floor system in the concrete slab.

After Hank Louis sold his grain-silo-turned-home-office, the next owner broadcast a radio show from the building. It is now owned by a landscape architect.

heating. Then they bolted together the first of six metal rings. To this first ring they then bolted the roof sections and the top band of galvanized siding. Around the bottom of the siding they affixed another metal ring. Then they lifted the whole section up on industrial jacks and attached the next band of siding along with the next metal ring. This construction process allows farmers to build up as high as they need to. Louis and his crew stopped at 25 ft.

Louis made the staircase out of a salvaged railroad trestle and hung the treads off the second-floor joists with metal rods. The rest of the space is an open plan, allowing desks and office furniture to go anywhere.

Elements like these walnut bookshelves show Louis's experimental style. The metal supports come from a steel tube that the crew cut and bent on site and the shelving is curved slightly to fit snug against the wall.

THE FLOATING CUBE

Once the exterior had been secured to the concrete slab, the architect made cutouts for windows and doors. Around the interior wall he built a wood frame to mimic the curve and to provide a cavity for insulation as well as rough openings for the windows and doors. The finished walls are made of ¼-in. maple veneer plywood that has been bent into place. Louis also built an open-sided cube inside the circular structure out of 8-ft. by 8-ft. posts, thereby providing the structure for the second floor. Because the upstairs is square with its corners just touching the sides of the silo, it has the appearance of a cube floating inside the building.

Louis has since sold his home and backyard office, but he misses working in the silo. Unlike the industrial steel exterior, the wood-paneled interior and a few unique built-in bookshelves lend it a much cozier feel. On days he wasn't teaching a morning class at the university he would get up before dawn to go to work alone. His desk faced the silo's windows because he enjoyed the view over Thaynes Canyon and the Park City ski area. These days everyone in town knows "the silo." Now if they'd only hire Louis to build them one of their own.

⚐ VICTORY LAP
STUDENT DESIGNED AND BUILT

The studio seminar Hank Louis teaches in the graduate department at the University of Utah's College of Architecture and Planning is more like a private firm than a class. It even has its own name—DesignBuildBLUFF—as well as independent funding from the U.S. Department of Housing and Urban Development. Working with low-income families on the Four Corners Navajo Reservation, students design and build affordable houses using salvaged materials, straw and rammed-earth walls, and passive solar site plans. Rainwater collection systems are standard, though no two houses ever look the same. Louis modeled DesignBuildBLUFF after Samuel Mockbee's Rural Studio, which designs and builds homes for the poor in Alabama.

TOY STORY

It has long been suspected that children's toys around the world are made by one man—with the help of some elves. But at 37 years old and with a slim build, Joe Masibay doesn't look anything like the guy in the white beard. Nor does he live at the North Pole. He lives in Harlem, where he designs toys in his 1,250-sq.-ft. apartment.

In New York City, 1,250 sq. ft. is a lot of room. Whereas some guys struggle to eke out a closet for themselves, Masibay had the luxury of choosing an entire bedroom for his studio. But then again, not many guys have as cool a job as his. Still, it wasn't always what he wanted to do. Growing up in Chicago, he was the type of kid who took apart the toaster to find out why it wasn't heating up. Only when he graduated college and got a job at a toy design company did he realize his true calling.

THE SMELL OF SPRAY PAINT IN THE MORNING

After a year and a half, Masibay left that job to follow his wife Kim to New York, where she had been accepted to Columbia Journalism School. There he decided to start his own business developing prototypes for toy companies.

Whether you're changing tires for a living or inventing toys, pegboard is the great equalizer. Masibay uses it to store his Jesus action figure and Nerf® gun.

This Barbie® telephone is just one of the toys Joe Masibay built in his Harlem apartment. When the phone rings, she twists and moves her arms to the music, just as the manufacturer wanted.

At first, he was commuting to a workspace on Long Island. When that proved too much trouble, he moved the operation into the Columbia University dorm room that he and Kim shared. He put a lathe and a drill mill (which acts as both a drill press and a milling machine) in the living room. When he needed to spray paint a completed model, he would sit by an open window using a fan. Eventually, they bought the three-bedroom, two-bathroom Harlem apartment they live in now.

Though Kim doesn't enjoy finding dirty tools in the spare bathroom sink, she is happy not to have to look at decapitated dolls strewn about the living room. Masibay has upgraded his tools to include a bandsaw and a computerized milling machine, which he keeps in a closet. To figure out the various mechanisms and gears for the models he makes, Masibay collects toys and dissects them like a scientist would a frog. He then uses his findings as examples and creates original gears for use in new toys, such as a Barbie phone (she starts dancing when it rings). Like all freelancers, Masibay has the luxury of working odd hours, but unlike that other toy guy, Joe takes Christmas off.

GEAR
TOOLS FOR TOYS

When Joe Masibay is creating a new toy car or robot arm he'll make a 3D design on a computer before actually carving it out of plastic or metal. He has a number of tools to help him do this, including a lathe and milling machine that can create any shape he wants using computer geometry. For fine-tuning a prototype he uses a combination drill press and milling machine (shown at left) that can perform both functions with a quick bit change. This "mini mill" is about 3 ft. high, weighs roughly 150 lb., and costs about $1,000.

Masibay collects toys to see how they work and to use as visual aids. Some, like the mini Vespa® scooter and the Hot Wheels®, he collects for fun.

A small bandsaw sits above Masibay's worktable, where he has been building a robot for a group of research scientists. When Masibay's inventing a new toy he's sworn to secrecy.

MANSPACE FOR YOUR HEALTH

Some men have to sneak, grab, or build their own spaces. Dave Paul was practically prescribed one by his doctor. After 15 years managing a company that organized international bicycle sightseeing tours, Paul was so exhausted that he checked himself into the hospital. Not long after Paul left the rat race, he and his wife moved to a 150-year-old house in the country.

For a year Paul didn't do much of anything, until he ran across a shop not far from his house that sold old canoes. For $300 he bought "an old wreck of a canoe" made out of wood that he decided to restore. Soon after, he enrolled in canoe-building workshops, then opened a canoe-repair business in a studio he built in his backyard.

At first, Paul would buy old canoes to fix up for resale. He enjoyed working with his hands and spending time in his workshop. He outfitted it with the typical conveniences of a weekender's woodworking studio, building a large rack suspended from the ceiling for wood storage. Built-in shelves and pegboard line the walls, where he stows handsaws, tack hammers, and clamps. To keep clutter to a minimum, Paul created a 24-ft. workbench along one wall.

After six years, Paul has become known in the area for his repair work. It still doesn't pay much, but his skills have improved greatly. In fact, to supplement the canoe restoration he has started refurbishing old wooden spinning wheels (his wife teaches spinning, so potentially there are a lot of clients). He's also taken a part-time job teaching at the local high school. Goodbye one rat race, hello another.

To taper a canoe rail, Dave Paul uses a specialized trim saw that helps the tool stay rigid and cut perfectly straight.

Because canoe building doesn't require heavy machinery, Paul's main gear is hand tools and clamps. He might use up to 20 clamps on one side of a canoe to help hold a new canvas in place.

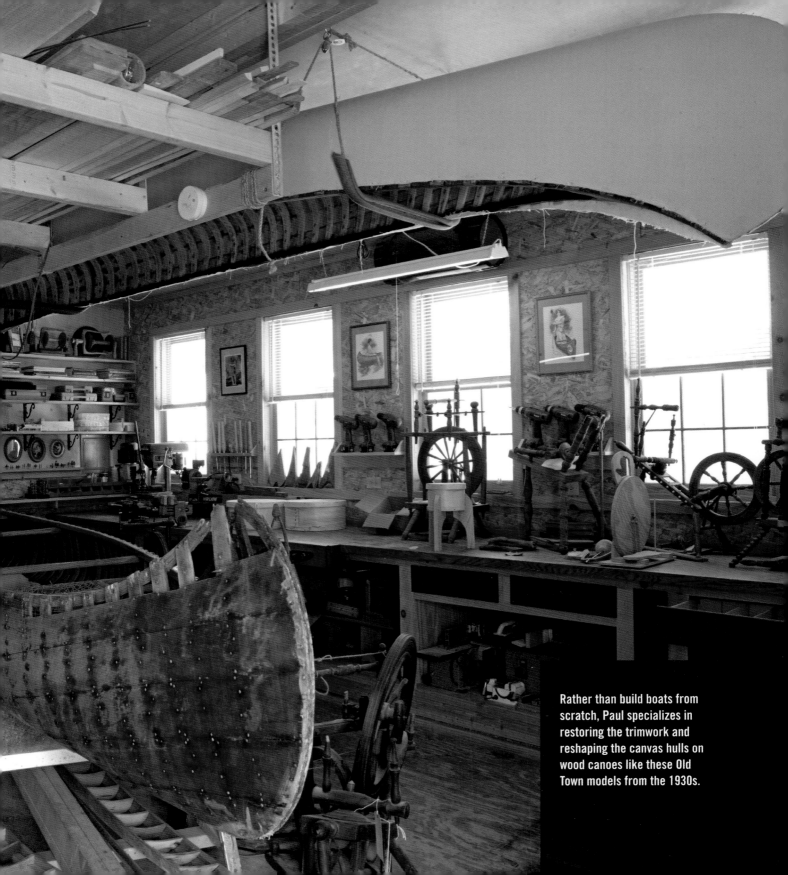

Rather than build boats from scratch, Paul specializes in restoring the trimwork and reshaping the canvas hulls on wood canoes like these Old Town models from the 1930s.

The beginning of a cedar decoy rests in a vice at Sarni's worktable. Duck bodies and heads are carved separately before being attached. The Glossy Ibis decoy with the long bill is all one piece.

CARVING OUT
A PLACE OF HIS OWN

Whittling a hunk of wood with a sharp knife has been a distinctly masculine urge for as long as there have been knives to whittle with. Decoy maker and retired structural engineer Bill Sarni has turned it into an art form. And now he has the dedicated space where he can fulfill his carving needs day or night.

Sarni's decoy-making workshop sits on a small bluff in the backyard of his home in Hingham, Mass. Though the barnlike building looks old, it was actually built three years ago. Students and teachers from Boston's famed North Bennet Street School spent a weekend at Sarni's

house erecting the authentic timber-frame structure—there isn't one nail in the northern white pine skeleton. Each mortise and tenon joint is locked in place with an oak pin.

Having his own space wasn't always the case. For 16 years Sarni carved his duck and shorebird decoys in a corner of his basement, which was also a playroom for his two daughters. To paint the carved birds he relocated upstairs to a table in the den. For years he considered renovating a dilapidated outbuilding on his property into a studio. Then he was invited to the North Bennet Street

Bill Sarni carves a decoy on the porch of his timber-frame workshop, carrying on the tradition of decoy makers from Hingham, Mass.

Bill Sarni's shop is almost entirely hand crafted, from the timber frame to the wood windows to the steel strap hinges on the barn doors that were cast from 19th-century originals by a friend.

School by a friend who was taking classes there—the students were preparing a timber-frame barn as part of an annual building project they erect for a lucky Boston local. As a structural engineer, Sarni had long been interested in timber-frame construction, so for him to see the timbers being cut and mortised using traditional techniques was a real treat. During his visit to the school he told one of the teachers that he'd love to have the school build one in his backyard. A week later he got his wish.

The diagonal timbers mortised and pinned into the ceiling joist and the wall post are called bents. They help brace the frame and keep the corner joints tight.

Sarni's tools include draw knives, wood rasps, and chisels of all sizes. Glue is used to attach the heads to the bodies, and paint brushes help finish the job.

FROM BASEMENT TO BARN

The building is 14 ft. by 24 ft., with an upstairs loft Sarni uses for storage and a 6-ft. by 24-ft. porch where he can carve in the summer months. After the frame was in place, Sarni hired two teachers and two students to put the roof on and finish the building. There is no insulation in the building—Sarni didn't want to cover up the interior framing and white pine walls. To keep warm in the winter he installed an oversize potbellied wood stove.

Now Sarni has plenty of space to spread out his carving knives and paint brushes, and he doesn't have to move everything into a different room in order to paint the finished birds. When he completes a decoy he sets it along with the others on the shelves he's built around the room so prospective buyers can come browse the inventory. He also posts images of them on his website, www.wdsdecoys.com. Sarni says the people buying his decoys are collectors rather than hunters, and he has three men who buy a dozen every year. Having loyal customers that appreciate the hard work and detail that goes into each decoy is one of Sarni's greatest rewards.

⃝ HOW STUFF WORKS
LEARNING THE TRADE

The North Bennet Street School students and teachers who constructed Bill Sarni's barn using 18th-century timber-framing techniques are part of a tradition that dates back more than 100 years. Established as a trade college in 1885, the Boston school teaches crafts ranging from bookbinding and jewelry making to violin restoration and preservation carpentry. The curriculum focuses on hands-on projects, and classes are small and intensive. Full-time students spend up to three years learning their trade, but the school also offers about 60 short workshops every year.

Man of Steel

1937 and was now dilapidated. Although its arched roof was caved in and it was filled with old cars, there was running water and a toilet. The Ringers bought the place for $6,700, parked the studio, and stayed.

FROM SCRAP TO SCULPTURE

In the late 1960s, Charlie Ringer's metal-working studio was a trailer he pulled behind the live-in van he shared with his wife Emily. It was stocked with grinders, welding equipment, and scrap metal. In the summer the couple would cruise the northern highways, and in the winter the southern ones, camping in spots for weeks at a time while Ringer made small metal silhouettes and sold them on the side of the highway.

One year, on a drive through Montana, Ringer and Emily spotted a "for sale" sign in front of a warehouse. The abandoned building had been a cheese factory in

The first order of business was to clear out a corner to live in. Then Ringer started making space for his tools. Cars were everywhere—103, to be exact. Because the local dump wouldn't take them whole, the Ringer's cut them up into pieces they could lift. It took six years. They also used car parts to remodel their living space, creating car chandeliers from headlights, building car windows into the walls, and bending mufflers into chairs. "Those were the starving artist days," says Ringer. "We had to make do with what we had."

Metal sculptor Charlie Ringer ignored the fact that the building he bought 35 years ago didn't have a roof. After living in a van for three years, a toilet that flushed was a major improvement.

Road signs, hub caps, and other metal memorabilia stock the walls of the building Ringer renovated in the early 1970s. He worked in his original studio—a former cheese factory—for 25 years. Now he mainly uses it to cut metal in.

The grounds of Ringer's compound store and exhibit "recollected" metal objects, including a dozen gas pumps, a 1901 metal truss bridge, a phone booth, and 70 cars.

In 2002 Ringer built himself a state-of-the-art metal shop with 15-ft. ceilings, a built-in gas-powered forge, radiant-floor heating, and laser cutters.

Ringer's bread and butter for many years in the studio was selling simple metal cutouts of covered wagons, old cars, cowboys, and farm animals.

It doesn't take long for found objects like these wheels, sprockets, and car parts to become sculpture at Ringer's metal shop.

He also made sculptures out of cars and other found objects. People began to stop on the highway and stroll down to have a look at the art. Some would buy it. In addition to his silhouettes of cowboys and wildlife, Ringer started creating business logos, furniture, and architectural elements like fireplace tools, hinges, hooks, and towel bars. The kinetic sculpture is made of interconnected pieces that move gently together.

Business eventually got so good that Ringer started buying the property around him. He bought a house behind the studio, which he and Emily and their three kids moved into. In 1995 he acquired a restaurant 300 feet down the highway and turned it into a gallery. In 2002 he bought five acres and a building next door to the original cheese factory. In the space between the arched-roof cheese factory and the newly acquired building next door, Ringer built a new brick studio with a board-and-batten shop front façade. He stocked it with the latest tools. He then connected all three buildings and turned the original space into his cutting room—still as useful as when he unloaded his van 35 years ago.

VICTORY LAP
MOVING SCULPTURE

A former hot-rod builder, Charlie Ringer knows how to weld metal so that it moves, though none of his sculptures go 0 to 60 mph in 5 seconds . . . yet. At this point his kinetic art takes a more poetic approach, rocking back and forth on an axle or twisting in the wind like a whimsical windmill. Some of these moveable masterpieces depict cowboys on horses or cows punched out in sheet metal like bullet holes in a stop sign. Others are geometric shapes welded to look like flowering bushes, abstract fans, or clocklike mandalas. Ringer's kinetic work ranges in size from 12-in. to 8-ft. tall and sells for $325 to $10,000.

SIZE MATTERS

If home is where a man hangs his hat, then Jay Shafer better not wear the ten-gallon variety. Before moving to California from Iowa last year, he built and lived in a 100-sq.-ft. house, complete with a porch. When he got to the West Coast he built a 70-sq.-ft. place. At 5 ft. 10 in., 130 lb., Shafer is a medium-size man and he does not own a hat.

Shafer's first tiny house came about while he was living small in an Airstream® trailer and decided to build a new house. During the design phase, he kept lopping off rooms and unnecessary square footage. His reasoning was that he really only needed a table to write and eat on and a place to sleep. In the end his blueprints showed an 8-ft. by 12-ft. gabled home with a loft bedroom, a bathroom, a kitchen, and a living room. To retain the sense of mobility he had with the Airstream (and to get around local building codes), Shafer added wheels.

The home cost him $15,000 in materials and took two mistake-filled years to build. Along the way he taught himself construction (the house is all standard stick framing and finishes). Even before Shafer had the last nail in, folks were marveling at the smallness of the place. In response, Shafer started selling the plans. He then came up with several more tiny house plans and opened a business called the Tumbleweed Tiny House Company. Now he builds homes full time for a growing number of small, medium, and large people who use them both as offices and as homes. Hats are not recommended.

STOVE

TOILET

KITCHEN

PROPANE STOVE

STORAGE CABINET

DESK

CHAIR

PORCH

With his tiny house, Jay Shafer wanted to make a statement about the wastefulness of oversize homes. And he didn't want to be saddled with too much housecleaning.

When not in use, Shafer's table folds up and stores behind the chair. Above the front door is the entry to the sleeping loft, which is accessible by ladder.

Unlike Shafer's newer tiny houses, this one has no plumbing; the bathroom is a closetlike 3 ft. by 3 ft. and features a composting toilet and a gravity-fed shower.

The kitchen to the right of the wood stove measures 3 ft. by 4 ft. and includes a two-burner propane cooktop and a sink. Gravity-fed water comes from a six-gallon tank.

A Master's Workshop

Where a man works is almost always as important as what he does. Take master woodworker Rick Schneider. When he built his Vermont studio he was happy just to have a room for power tools rather than the loft apartment he lived and worked in. But today, as a widely sought-after woodworker, he and his space have achieved something of celebrity status. In 1998 Schneider appeared on the Discovery Channel, and in 2002 he was part of HGTV's modern masters series. Both productions filmed inside his studio to show his tools and setup. They were also interested in the studio.

Schneider built the barnlike structure in 1977 using passive solar design so that the sun—rather than a heating system—would heat the building in the winter. One large bank of windows on the southern wall draws enough sunlight to light and warm the space even in the brutal Vermont winters. Deciduous trees planted outside the windows let the sun in during the winter and shade the windows during the summers to keep the interior cool. The windows also open to allow the prevailing winds to ventilate the room. No air conditioning is necessary.

Rick Schneider's woodshop has 15-ft. ceilings to accommodate his spiral staircases, as well as plywood floors that he can drill into or attach things to.

Schneider carves a lily blossom using an enlarged photograph of an earlier flower sculpture as a guide. Works in progress are mounted on a carving board that swivels and rotates up to a 90° angle.

Two of Schneider's lily blossom sculptures and a miniature spiral staircase model rest on the tread of a partially finished project. A carving board in the background is angled up off its base.

FUNCTIONAL ARTWORK

The design has been so user-friendly over the years that Schneider hasn't had to change a thing. Instead, he's been able to concentrate on woodworking. Like the furniture he creates, his spiral staircases are "functional pieces of art." They're built entirely out of solid wood, like cherry or maple. Often the winding stair railing is made from a single piece of lumber, hand carved over thousands of hours. When he isn't building staircases, he's working on sculptures or carved architectural details. The

basswood pineapples carved on the ceiling of the Vermont statehouse were lovingly hand-rendered by Schneider.

Unlike lots of guys who work in backyard offices or spare bedrooms, Schneider has a bit of a commute—200 yd. to be exact. In the summer the flower-lined path from his cabin where he lives with his wife is a pleasant stroll. When the snow is deep, the path becomes a cross country ski run. Either way it's a commute Schneider still looks forward to every morning.

Schneider built his barnlike studio in 1977 on property his parents bought in the late 1960s. Double doors swing wide to accommodate the woodworker's staircases and large sculptures.

Living with the Lost Arts

Thirteen years ago Richard Spreda's blacksmith shop was a run-down old barn in the village center of Stowe, Vt. The floor was made of dirt, except where a few logs covered a cellar toward the back of the building. Upstairs, the second-story hayloft was filled with spiders and dust.

When Spreda came along and said he'd buy the place, people told him he was wasting his money. But beyond the dilapidation, the burly former excavating contractor envisioned a glowing forge and the black steel face of his blacksmith's anvil filling the space with the din of his hard work. Blacksmithing had been Spreda's hobby for years as he shaped his own horseshoes while playing indoor arena polo. It was time to pursue it full time.

First, he renovated the cellar apartment. Spreda dug out the dirt floor in the main building and cellar until he reached ledge stone. Then he installed radiant-floor tubing and poured concrete slabs. Next he roughed in the plumbing for the entire building, then installed a small bathroom and a kitchenette. The hayloft would be his living space.

FORGING A LIVING SPACE

Doing most of the work himself, he constructed a huge brick chimney on the far side of the building. He put in three flues, including one for the forge. He reinforced the floor of the hayloft with a steel I-beam and installed

The blacksmith calls the bathroom one of his favorite rooms in the house. He has a soaking tub to wash off the day's soot and plenty of cabinets to store toiletries.

Richard Spreda's blacksmith shop in the village center of Stowe, Vt., is a popular stop for tourists. "Sometimes they come to buy but mostly it's to tell me that their grandfather was a blacksmith," he says.

Spreda mostly uses the tiny loft in his 750-sq.-ft. apartment for storage, though his daughter slept there when she was a student at a nearby college.

another concrete floor with radiant heat. The beam also serves as a track for a small crane in the forge so that he can move heavy materials.

To finish out the 750-sq.-ft. second-floor apartment he hired carpenters. An avid sailor, he wasn't worried about the compact space, creating boatlike interior elements such as the built-in cabinets in the bathroom and the bedroom and the bowed ceiling above the kitchen. Painted plywood covers the floor, and curved pieces of wood line the interior roof ridge to mimic the concave hull of a boat.

Spreda rents out the cellar apartment and has built several terraces on the hillside out back where he can work in good weather. His shop has two employees and together they craft metal sculpture, door handles, fireplace tools, chairs, tables, and chandeliers. The only thing not for sale is the life he's painstakingly forged for himself.

Blacksmithing isn't Spreda's only skill—he's also a handy cook. Thus the restaurant-style stove in the tiny kitchen.

DAVID WILD'S BRAIN

It is both a blessing and curse that creative types spend a lot of time in their own heads. On the one hand, it's nice to always have a place to set up shop—men who have no physical digs should take note. On the other hand, if that's the only place a man has to go, things can get a little cluttered. That's when the headspace needs to be vacated in favor of something less contemplative, like going for a jog or watching a good car-chase movie.

Filmmaker David Wild came up with an even better solution: He built a replica of his brain in his backyard. When he needs to work on a script or edit a commercial,

he walks 40 steps from his main house to The Brain and gets to work.

Wild hasn't always had the luxury of working in a posh modern building like his backyard brain. For most of the past 20 years he worked out of a variety of small apartments in Michigan and Los Angeles (in addition to creating some original short films, Wild directs commercials for Nike® and Saturn®, among others). When he and his wife Lulu moved to Seattle several years ago, he kept his books and inspirational scraps of daily life in the main house—not the best arrangement, according to Lulu. So the couple decided to build a two-car garage and a studio where Wild could think more clearly.

The modern building is much better looking than the actual gray matter stuffed between Wild's ears. It does, however, include plenty of comparable quirks. Designed by architect Tom Kundig of Olson Sundberg Kundig Allen

When construction on The Brain was finished, Wild worried that the place was so cool he wouldn't have any more excuses for not being able to come up with new ideas.

Wild says the most novel thing about having a studio separate from his house is that it keeps him organized. From his desk in the loft his ideas literally take flight.

David Wild's studio offers a space for the filmmaker to go sit with his thoughts or tease them out.

10 03

Three industrial-looking pulleys hanging from the ceiling raise bare lightbulbs to the top of the 16-ft. ceilings or lower them right to the hardwood floor.

The steel stairs to the loft were so slippery that the architects decided to weld on some treads. Wild suggested an adage his father used to say.

A man's got to feed his brain. Wild teases out a phrase or two at the piano to get the creative juices flowing.

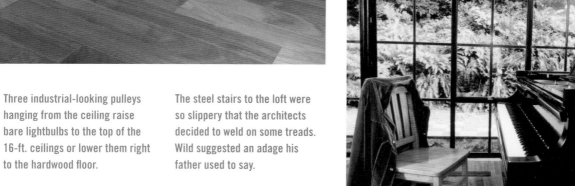

Architects, the 900-sq.-ft. think tank has no parallel walls—even the ceiling slopes from 16 ft. to 18 ft. The industrialized interior is one giant room with concrete walls, pulleys, and bare lightbulbs hanging from the ceiling and a tunnel of light bored through its center by two 16-ft. by 16-ft. windows. On one side of the room is a bank of bookshelves, a darkroom, and a loft. Once before, when he was living in Michigan, the filmmaker had a "dank and cluttered" workshop "like the inside of [his] head" that he used to call "The Brain." His instructions to Kundig were to build him another heady space and the name stuck.

Just as The Brain isn't a typical office space, Wild isn't a typical office denizen. One of the things he likes to do when he writes is put a CD on and repeat it for eight hours with the volume on high. For him the music becomes a mantra to block the outside world. In fact, everything in the studio is there to inspire the filmmaker to come up with clever new ideas and have fun while he does it. To unclog a momentary onset of writer's block he might play the piano, slide down a fire pole, or fondle his collection of throwing knives. Perhaps unlike many creatives, Wild never tires of spending too much time in his Brain.

HOW STUFF WORKS
GRAY MATTER BY DESIGN

Architect Tom Kundig of Olson Sundberg Kundig Allen Architects in Seattle knew there would be a lot of creative thinking going on inside the studio he was designing for David Wild, so he made sure the building itself would inspire. The structure is essentially a cast-in-place concrete box with 8-in.-thick walls and a stark interior. The sides and the top, however, taper in at one end and the ceiling slopes gently from one side to the next. This gives the interior excellent acoustic qualities for Wild, who plays the piano and listens to lots of music.

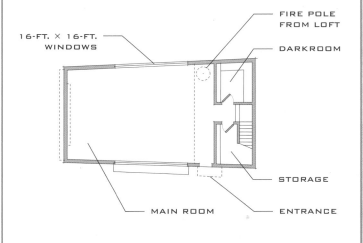

16-FT. × 16-FT. WINDOWS

FIRE POLE FROM LOFT

DARKROOM

STORAGE

MAIN ROOM

ENTRANCE

Married, with Manspace

Lots of married men need to separate their work from their family life. Bill Kerby needs more than that. In fact, when he and his wife Paula got married they never even tried living together without a dedicated space for Bill. That's because these self-proclaimed loners knew that when they tied the knot in middle age the only way the relationship was going to work was if they could spend as much time apart from each other as they needed. Their solution was to buy a house with a backyard cabin. Bill, who is a film and television writer, uses the cabin to work on screenplays, watch TV, read, and feed his dog. Paula spends her days in the main house. For all practical purposes, the two have separate residences on the same piece of property—Bill even crashes in the cabin's loft bedroom on some nights.

Architect Ross Chapin designed and built the house, the cabin, and the "pocket neighborhood" where the Kerbys live. His idea for the extra 425-sq.-ft. cabin was to create a separate living space for in-laws, guests, or children home from college. The two-room building has a loft, a bathroom, a kitchen alcove, an eating nook, and radiant floor heating. Bill's cabin is an office and repository for his books and odd assortment of furniture, including a barber's chair and a stool made out of a tomato-red tractor seat. Paula was happy to let him have the last two items.

The entrance to Kerby's private cabin is 200 ft. from the main house, but it's far from any kind of disturbance.

Kerby is the author of several movie scripts, the most famous of which is the 1979 feature *The Rose,* staring Bette Midler.

Bill Kerby's backyard writing cabin is loaded with books, trains, and other knickknacks he uses as inspiration for his writing projects.

A typical day for Bill has him up early for a six-mile walk, then back to the cabin to drink coffee and watch the television programs he taped the night before. He'll then sit down at his desk to work. Bill might see Paula a few times a day; otherwise, the two spend enough time apart to have a healthy relationship.

Kerby's dining alcove doubles as a stereo table and reading nook. Comfort is one of the writer's main sources of inspiration.

On the wall of Kerby's office is a ladder leading to the loft bed and framed awards he's won during his 35-year career writing for television and film.

Kerby's barber chair was originally in the main house until his wife Paula banished it to the cabin.

Ned Thompson's favorite time to be in his riverfront woodshop is the fall, when he can have a football game on while working on a project—in this case a boat model.

Waterfront Woodshop

Ned Thompson's wife Margo never liked the woodshop Ned kept for 23 years in their Portsmouth home's basement. Every time he cut something, sawdust would seep up through the old floorboards. Ned, who owns a company that manufactures canvas, wasn't thrilled about the space either. It was dark and he didn't like hiding himself away when he wanted to indulge in his hobby, which was several times a week. When they moved across town to an 18th-century colonial on the Piscataqua River, both the Thompsons were much happier. Ned got a small but

bright outbuilding that he could happily renovate into a woodshop. Margo got a dust-free house.

The outbuilding was built in the 1920s and used to store the previous owner's equipment—he was a boat builder. It had been constructed on top of a dock and a third of it was cantilevered over the river. By the time Ned got it, the building and its foundation were in such bad repair that he was afraid the whole thing might fall into the water. The slab was cracked and broken. Panes of glass were missing, and cardboard had been tacked up to block the weather. Also, the building's studs were badly deteriorated and had to be completely replaced—all typical for a building so close to the water but no less disconcerting.

The first thing Ned did was remove the cracked foundation and pour a new one with radiant-heating tubes. To ensure the cantilevered building would remain on dry

Thompson's woodshop, which his wife lovingly calls "Ned's Shed," also houses an upstairs office for the couple.

All Thompson's power tools, including this drill press (on left) and bandsaw, are on castors to make them easy to roll out of the way.

Thompson likes to say that his clamps are "another set of hands." He's found that 2×4s with holes drilled in them and attached to the ceiling make great clamp holders.

Efficient space-saving features make Thompson's small shop workable. A single cabinet houses both his planer and his joiner. PVC pipes above the door hold dowels, spare molding, and piping.

Paint cans hang up and out of the way above the sink, next to which is one of Thompson's projects: a birdhouse replica of the Portsmouth Children's Museum.

ground, he made the slab 8 in. thick. After replacing the framing studs, Ned added a second-floor office, then he wired the building with extra outlets for his power tools. Because the space was so small—320 sq. ft. in total—Ned made sure his workbench, his power tools, and even his wood-storage bin were on wheels to be easily moved out of the way. He also made drawers, cabinets, brackets, and a few of his own creations to store his tools and materials.

Now Ned spends several evenings a week and every Sunday in his workshop, happily piecing together projects that range from birdhouses to built-ins for a sailboat he keeps moored at the end of the dock. He's close to the neighborhood road, so friends often stop by to chat when they see the lights on in the workshop. Unlike the basement he used to work in, his new space allows him to see anyone coming and going. It's like having a room to himself and being able to keep an eye on everything else at the same time.

HOW STUFF WORKS
SMALL SPACE STORAGE

"It has to be easy to put things away or else things will end up strewn all over the place," Ned Thompson says of his small workspace. So he created the "jar wheel," a six-sided length of wood to which lids are screwed and jars attached to hold nails, pins, nuts, and wood screws. The wheel is attached to the ceiling and can be rotated. Another simple invention is a wooden bracket to store spray-paint cans on their sides to better see the color-coated tops. Easy access means easy cleanup.

RESOURCES

STUFF

SERVICES